The Ultimate
Book of Insults

The Ultimate
Book of Insults

Geoff Tibballs

Magpie, London

Constable & Robinson Ltd
3 The Lanchesters
162 Fulham Palace Road
London W6 9ER

This edition published by Magpie Books,
an imprint of Constable & Robinson Ltd 2006

A copy of the British Library Cataloguing in Publication Data
is available from the British Library

ISBN 10: 1-84529-451-3
ISBN 13: 978-1-84529-451-9

Printed and bound in the European Union

1 3 5 7 9 10 8 6 4 2

Contents

Contents

Famous Put-Downs

Art

Junk masquerading as art.
ANON, of Tracey Emin

Walt Whitman is as unacquainted with art as a hog with mathematics.
ANON

Paul Klee's pictures seem to resemble, not pictures, but a sample book of patterns of linoleum.
CYRIL ASQUITH

The only major influence on [Francis] Bacon has been his own surname.
JULIAN BARNES

I'd like to wring the fellow's neck.
PAUL CÉZANNE, of Paul Gauguin

[Edgar] Degas is nothing but a peeping Tom, behind the *coulisses*, and among the dressing-rooms of the ballet dancers, noting only travesties of fallen debased womanhood.
THE CHURCHMAN

For 1,000 years art has been one of our great civilising forces. Today, pickled sheep and soiled beds threaten to make barbarians of us all.
DAILY MAIL, of Damien Hirst

A catastrophe of awkwardness – a painter of decrepit structures of the past.
SALVADOR DALI, of Paul Cézanne

A skilful but short-lived decorator.
EDGAR DEGAS, of Claude Monet

Dada's art is just turpentine intoxication.
MARCEL DUCHAMP

Sister Wendy is to art what Saint Teresa was to sex education.
A.A. GILL

If landscape can be satisfactorily painted without either drawing or colour, [Charles] Daubigny is the man to do it.
P.G. HAMERTON

Why did you paint it so large? A small canvas might have concealed your faults.
WILLIAM HAZLITT, of a painting by Benjamin Haydon

He only recognises art with his wallet.
DAMIEN HIRST, of Charles Saatchi

The properties of his figures are sometimes such as might be corrected by a common sign-painter.
WILLIAM HOGARTH, of Antonio Correggio

Many painters and writers have made beautiful works out of repulsive objects; Picasso enjoys making repulsive works out of beautiful objects.
RAYMOND MORTIMER

[Edouard] Manet must be the greatest and most uncritical ass who ever lived.
DANTE GABRIEL ROSSETTI

Ignorant, inarticulate, talentless, loutish.
BRIAN SEWELL, of Tracey Emin

It is no more interesting than a stuffed pike over a pub door. Indeed there may well be more art in a stuffed pike than a dead sheep.
BRIAN SEWELL, of Damien Hirst's pickled sheep

She deserves better than to be perpetuated as an old age pensioner about to lose her bungalow.
BRIAN SEWELL, of Anthony Williams's portrait of Queen Elizabeth II for her seventieth birthday

Cézanne was fated, as his passion was immense, to be immensely neglected, immensely misunderstood, and now I think, immensely overrated.
WALTER SICKERT

Mr [Wyndham] Lewis's pictures appeared to have been painted by a mailed fist in a cotton glove.
EDITH SITWELL

Art needs [John] Ruskin like a moving train needs one of the passengers to shove it.
TOM STOPPARD

If Botticelli were alive today, he'd be working for *Vogue*.
PETER USTINOV

The only genius with an IQ of sixty.
GORE VIDAL, of Andy Warhol

A monstrous orchid.
OSCAR WILDE, of Aubrey Beardsley

With our James [Whistler] vulgarity begins at home, and should be allowed to stay there.
OSCAR WILDE

The only thoroughly original ideas I have ever heard him express have had reference to his own superiority as a painter over painters greater than himself.
OSCAR WILDE, of James Whistler

For that he is indeed one of the very greatest masters of painting, is my opinion. And I may add that in this opinion Mr Whistler himself entirely concurs.
OSCAR WILDE, of James Whistler

Just explain to Monsieur Renoir that the torso of a woman is not a mass of decomposing flesh, its green and violet spots indicating the state of complete putrefaction of a corpse.
ALBERT WOLFF

Dorothy Todd is like a slug with a bleeding gash for a mouth.
VIRGINIA WOOLF

To convince Cézanne of anything is like teaching the towers of Nôtre Dame to dance.
EMILE ZOLA

Celebrity

Vanessa [Feltz] is hardly riveting. Indeed watching riveting would make for better television.
ANON

Loyd Grossman suffers from irritable vowel syndrome.
ANON

Who let the dogs out? Woof, woof.
VICTORIA BECKHAM, to Jordan

Arianna Stassinopoulos is so boring you fall asleep halfway through her name.
ALAN BENNETT

This is one Hilton that should be closed for renovation.
MR BLACKWELL, of Paris Hilton

Anna Nicole Smith looks like a rag doll trapped in a wind machine.
MR BLACKWELL

I'm never going to be as skinny as Posh. And I hope people don't think I sing like her either. That would be a bit worrying.
CHARLOTTE CHURCH, of Victoria Beckham

David Blaine is scruffy and can't be bothered to get dressed up. He's wearing what a bum on the street would wear.
PAUL DANIELS

It doesn't matter how gym-toned the girl might be, there is still something about her that looks like she was designed to bring in the washing.
JENNY ÉCLAIR, of Coleen McLoughlin

Mocking Hugh Hefner is easy to do, and in my mind should be made easier.
CLIVE JAMES

She'll never be as big as me – look at her nose and her boobs, she's ugly.
JORDAN, of Jodie Marsh

As you know, Tom Cruise and Katie Holmes had a baby girl. It weighs seven pounds seven ounces and is twenty inches long . . . wait, that's Tom.
DAVID LETTERMAN

What first attracted you to the millionaire Paul Daniels?
MRS MERTON, to Debbie McGee

Like the Queen, only grander.
ALLISON PEARSON, of Heather Mills McCartney

My first reaction on hearing that David Beckham may have been playing away with his former PA, Rebecca Loos, was who could blame the poor soul?
AMANDA PLATELL

Victoria Beckham is to women about as real as Tanya in *Footballers' Wives*. But more calculating. The only real thing about her is her ambition.
AMANDA PLATELL

Jade Goody's the only woman I can think of who always makes the rest of us feel slim, fit and talented.
AMANDA PLATELL

That's the kind of face you hang on your door in Africa.
JOAN RIVERS, of Donatella Versace

Are we so starved of entertainment that we are entertained by a trickless magician sitting in a box for forty-four days with no food?
CHRIS ROCK, of David Blaine

Was there a star in the East when this self-worshipping little man was born?
JEAN ROOK, of Eric Morley

Comedy

Jack Benny's so cheap he wouldn't give you the parsley off his fish.
FRED ALLEN

Lucille Ball was to comedy what Vanessa Feltz is to hang-gliding.
ANON

A man whose comedic talent is limited to pulling faces.
ANON, of Jim Carrey

Laugh? I nearly started.
ANON, of Jim Davidson

Bobby Davro's career is now so far off course he doesn't need an agent, he needs a St Bernard.
GARRY BUSHELL

Occasionally funny, usually superficial, always pompous.
BOBBY DARIN, of Bob Hope

I don't really find any silent comedians funny. I don't identify with it. I've never had to wallpaper a room while delivering a piano upstairs.
ANGUS DEAYTON

Steve Martin has basically one joke and he's it.
DAVE FELTON

Groucho Marx is a male chauvinistic piglet.
BETTY FRIEDAN

Robin Williams's technique is to say 500 things with a joke rhythm, and at least two of them might be funny.
LIBBY GELMAN-WAXNER

Jennifer Saunders is a one-trick horse; Dawn French is a one-trick carthorse.
A.A. GILL

Sandra Bernard is as much fun as barbed wire.
TOM HUTCHINSON

Bob Hope is a funny guy, but if he was drowning he couldn't ad lib "Help!"
HAL KANTER

I treasure every moment that I do not see her.
OSCAR LEVANT, of Phyllis Diller

Jimmy Tarbuck doesn't tell gags – he just refreshes your memory.
BERNARD MANNING

Milton Berle is an inspiration to every young person that wants to get into show business. Hard work, perseverance, and discipline: all the things you need when you have no talent.
DEAN MARTIN

[Bob] Hope is not a comedian. He just translates what others write for him.
GROUCHO MARX

Over the past fifty years Bob Hope employed eighty-eight joke writers who supplied him with more than one million gags. And he still couldn't make me laugh.
EDDIE MURPHY

Joan Rivers's face hasn't just had a lift, it's taken the elevator all the way to the top floor without stopping.
CLIVE JAMES

The man was a major comedian, which is to say that he had the compassion of an icicle, the effrontery of a carnival shrill, and the generosity of a pawnbroker.
S.J. PERELMAN, of Groucho Marx

The amount of money he's earned for not making me laugh is staggering.
WILL SELF, of Frank Skinner

Phyllis Diller's so ancient she's just a carcass with a mouth.
RUBY WAX

Literature

He writes so well he makes me feel like putting the quill back in the goose.
FRED ALLEN, of an unnamed author

A huge pendulum attached to a small clock.
ANON, of Samuel Taylor Coleridge

There was little about melancholy that he didn't know; there was little else that he did.
W. H. AUDEN, of Alfred, Lord Tennyson

Frankly I would prefer to read a novel about civil servants written by a rabbit.
CRAIG BROWN, of Richard Adams's *Watership Down*

Is there no beginning to your talents?
CLIVE ANDERSON, to Jeffrey Archer

Thank you for sending me a copy of your book. I'll waste no time reading it.
ANON

I have only been mildly bored.
GERTRUDE ATHERTON, after a lengthy debate with Ambrose
Bierce

A fat flabby little person with the face of a baker, the
clothes of a cobbler, the size of a barrelmaker, the manners
of a stocking salesman and the dress of an innkeeper.
VICTOR DE BALABIN, of Honoré de Balzac

You ought to be roasted alive: though even then, you would
not be to my taste.
J. M. BARRIE, to George Bernard Shaw

I've read some of your modern free verse and wonder who
set it free.
JOHN BARRYMORE, to an unnamed poet

She is stupid, heavy and garrulous. She has good reasons to
wish to abolish Hell.
CHARLES BAUDELAIRE, of George Sand

Byron! He would be all forgotten today if he had lived to be a
florid old gentleman with iron-grey whiskers writing very
long, very able letters to *The Times* about the repeal of the
Corn Laws.
MAX BEERBOHM

George Bernard Shaw uses the English language like a
truncheon.
MAX BEERBOHM

The covers of this book are too far apart.
AMBROSE BIERCE

The sovereign of insufferables. He had nothing to say and he said it.
AMBROSE BIERCE, of Oscar Wilde

You can gain nothing by reading her. It is like eating snowballs, with which one can surfeit one's self without satisfying the stomach.
NAPOLEON BONAPARTE, of Marie de Sevigne

The stupid person's idea of a clever person.
ELIZABETH BOWEN, of Aldous Huxley

Henry Miller is not really a writer but a non-stop talker to whom someone has given a typewriter.
GERALD BRENAN

[Henry Wadsworth] Longfellow is to poetry what the barrel-organ is to music.
VAN WYCK BROOKS

Balzac was so conceited that he raised his hat every time he spoke of himself.
ROBERT BROUGHTON

The "g" is silent – the only thing about her that is.
JULIE BURCHILL, of Camille Paglia

I knew William Faulkner well. He was a great friend of mine. Well, much as you could be a friend of his, unless you were a fourteen-year-old nymphet.
TRUMAN CAPOTE

Jacqueline Susann looks like a truck driver in drag.
TRUMAN CAPOTE

I guess Gore [Vidal] left the country because he felt he was
under-appreciated here. I have news for him: people who
actually read his books will under-appreciate him everywhere.
TRUMAN CAPOTE

Never did I see such apparatus got ready for thinking, and
never so little thought. He mounts scaffolding, pulleys, and
tackles, gathers all the tools in the neighbourhood with
labour, with noise, demonstration, precept, and sets – three
bricks.
THOMAS CARLYLE, of Samuel Taylor Coleridge

Poor [Percy Bysshe] Shelley always was, and is, a kind of
ghastly object; colourless, pallid, tuneless, without health
or warmth or vigour.
THOMAS CARLYLE

Sitting in a sewer and adding to it.
THOMAS CARLYLE, of Algernon Charles Swinburne

[George Bernard] Shaw's brain is a half-inch layer of
champagne poured over a bucket of Methodist near-beer.
BENJAMIN DE CASSERES

Silly, snobbish, lecherous, tipsy, given to high-flown sentiments and more than a little humbug...Öhe needed Johnson
as ivy needs an oak.
CYRIL CONNOLLY, of James Boswell

He would not blow his nose without moralising on the conditions in the handkerchief industry.
CYRIL CONNOLLY, of George Orwell

She looked like Lady Chatterley above the waist and the gamekeeper below.
CYRIL CONNOLLY, of Vita Sackville-West

The world is rid of Lord Byron, but the deadly slime of his touch still remains.
JOHN CONSTABLE

Frankly, I should bury it in a drawer and put a lily on it.
NOËL COWARD, of a friend's first short story

What a tiresome, affected sod.
NOËL COWARD, of Oscar Wilde

Your Majesty, do not hang George Wither lest it be said that I am the worst poet in the kingdom.
JOHN DENHAM

He never wrote an invitation to dinner without an eye to posterity.
BENJAMIN DISRAELI, of Edward Bulwer-Lytton

Robert Benchley has a style that is weak and lies down frequently to rest.
MAX EASTMAN

I wish her characters would talk a little less like the heroes and heroines of police reports.
GEORGE ELIOT, of Charlotte Brontë

Of Byron one can say, as of no other English poet of his eminence, that he added nothing to the language, that he discovered nothing in the sounds, and developed nothing in the meaning of individual words.
T.S. ELIOT

Henry James had a mind so fine that no idea could violate it.
T.S. ELIOT

[Alfred Lord] Tennyson is a beautiful half of a poet.
RALPH WALDO EMERSON

A bell with a wooden tongue.
RALPH WALDO EMERSON, of William Wordsworth

Gertrude Stein was a master at making nothing happen very slowly.
CLIFTON FADIMAN

Ernest Hemingway has never been known to use a word that might send the reader to a dictionary.
WILLIAM FAULKNER

One of the nicest old ladies I ever met.
WILLIAM FAULKNER, of Henry James

A hack writer who would have been considered fourth rate in Europe, who tried out a few of the old proven "sure-fire" literary skeletons with sufficient local colour to intrigue the superficial and the lazy.
WILLIAM FAULKNER, of Mark Twain

Always willing to lend a helping hand to the one above him.
F. SCOTT FITZGERALD, of Ernest Hemingway

What an old covered wagon she is.
F. SCOTT FITZGERALD, of Gertrude Stein

Lord Byron writes with the thoughts of a city clerk in metropolitan clerical vernacular.
FORD MADOX FORD

[Joseph] Conrad spent a day finding the *mot juste*; then killed it.
FORD MADOX FORD

Listening to Alexander Woollcott is like being hit with a cream puff; you are uninjured but rather sickened.
ROBERT FORSYTHE

Obsessed with self. Dead eyes and a red beard, long narrow face. A strange bird.
JOHN GALSWORTHY, of D.H. Lawrence

There is no arguing with [Samuel] Johnson; for when his pistol misses fire, he knocks you down with the butt end of it.
OLIVER GOLDSMITH

To me, [Ezra] Pound remains the exquisite showman minus the show.
BEN HECHT

[Johann Ludwig] Uhland's poetry is like the famous war horse, Bayard; it possesses all possible virtues and only one fault – it is dead.
HEINRICH HEINE

Poor [William] Faulkner. Does he really think emotions come from big words?
ERNEST HEMINGWAY

George Eliot: a fungus of pendulous shape.
ALICE JAMES

Barbara Cartland's eyes were twin miracles of mascara and looked like two small crows that had crashed into a chalk cliff.
CLIVE JAMES

He was dull in company, dull in his closet, dull everywhere. He was dull in a new way and that made people think him great.
SAMUEL JOHNSON, of Thomas Gray

We have met too late. You are too old for me to have any effect on you.
JAMES JOYCE, to W. B. Yeats

[William] Wordsworth has left a bad impression wherever he visited in town by his egotism, vanity and bigotry.
JOHN KEATS

He grew up from manhood into boyhood.
R.A. KNOX, of G.K. Chesterton

Dank, limber verses, stuft with lakeside sedges
And propt with rotten stakes from rotten hedges.
WALTER SAVAGE LANDOR, of William Wordsworth

Gertrude Stein's prose is a cold, black suet-pudding. We can represent it as a cold suet-roll of fabulously reptilian length. Cut it at any point, it is the same heavy, sticky, opaque mass all through, and all along.
WYNDHAM LEWIS

It is a better thing to be a starved apothecary than a starved poet. So back to the shop, Mr John. Back to plaster, pills and ointment boxes.
J.G. LOCKHART, of John Keats

All the faults of *Jane Eyre* are magnified thousandfold and the only consolation which we have in reflecting upon it, is that it will never be generally read.
JAMES LORIMER, of Emily Brontë's *Wuthering Heights*

Every word she writes is a lie, including "and" and "the".
MARY MCCARTHY, of Lillian Hellman

His imagination resembles the wings of an ostrich.
THOMAS BABINGTON MACAULAY, of John Dryden

The more I read Socrates, the less I wonder they poisoned him.
THOMAS BABINGTON MACAULAY

The greatest mind ever to stay in prep school.
NORMAN MAILER, of J.D. Salinger

E.M. Forster never gets any further than warming the teapot. He's a rare fine hand at that. Feel this teapot. Is it not beautifully warm? Yes, but there ain't going to be no tea.
KATHERINE MANSFIELD

The white and creamy look of an animated meringue.
ARTHUR MARSHALL, of Barbara Cartland

From the moment I picked up your book until I laid it down I was convulsed with laughter. Someday I intend reading it.
GROUCHO MARX, of a book by S.J. Perelman

Alexander Woollcott looked like something that had gotten loose from Macy's Thanksgiving Day Parade.
HARPO MARX

Henry James had turned his back on one of the great events in the world's history, the rise of the United States, in order to report tittle-tattle at tea parties in English country houses.
W. SOMERSET MAUGHAM

To hear W. B.Yeats read his own verses was as excruciating a torture as anyone could be exposed to.
W. SOMERSET MAUGHAM

Some call [Alexander] Pope little nightingale – all sound and no sense.
MARY WORTLEY MONTAGU

Cicero's style bores me. When I have spent an hour reading him and try to recollect what I have extracted, I usually find it nothing but wind.

MICHEL DE MONTAIGNE

What is [Joseph Conrad] but the wreck of Stevenson floating about in the slipslop of Henry James?

GEORGE MOORE

Probably [James] Joyce thinks that because he prints all the dirty little words he is a great hero.

GEORGE MOORE

Oscar Wilde's talent seems to me to be essentially rootless, something growing in glass on a little water.

GEORGE MOORE

Coleridge was a muddle-headed metaphysician who by some strange streak of fortune turned out a few poems amongst the dreary flood of inanity that was his wont.

WILLIAM MORRIS

[Rudyard] Kipling is a jingo imperialist, he is morally insensitive and aesthetically disgusting.

GEORGE ORWELL

The affair between Margot Asquith and Margot Asquith will live as one of the prettiest love stories in all literature.

DOROTHY PARKER

This is not a novel to be tossed aside lightly. It should be thrown with great force.

DOROTHY PARKER

Mr [William] Wordsworth, a stupid man, with a decided gift for portraying nature in vignettes, never ruined anyone's morals, unless, perhaps, he has driven some susceptible persons to crime in a very fury of boredom.
EZRA POUND

An overgrown pimple, sore to the touch.
QUARTERLY REVIEW, of William Hazlitt

[Wilfred] Owen's tiny corpus is perhaps the most overrated poetry in the twentieth century.
CRAIG RAINE

To say [Agatha] Christie's characters are cardboard cut-outs is an insult to cardboard.
RUTH RENDELL

Very nice, though there are dull stretches.
ANTOINE DE RIVAROL, of a fellow writer's two-line poem

[William Makepeace] Thackeray settled like a meat-fly on whatever one had got for dinner, and made one sick of it.
JOHN RUSKIN

Waldo [Ralph Waldo Emerson] is one of those people who would be enormously improved by death.
SAKI

Jane Austen's novels, which strangely retain their hold on the public taste, are tedious to those who dare to think for themselves.
KATE SANBORN

He has never played any significant part in any movement more significant than that of a fly on a wheel.
SATURDAY REVIEW, of Charles Dickens

Concerning no subject would [George Bernard] Shaw be deterred by the minor accident of total ignorance from penning a definitive opinion.
ROGER SCRUTON

With the single exception of Homer, there is no eminent writer, not even Sir Walter Scott, whom I can despise so entirely as I despise Shakespeare when I measure my mind against his. It would positively be a relief for me to dig him up and throw stones at him.
GEORGE BERNARD SHAW

Living almost always among intellectuals, she preserved to the age of fifty-six that contempt for ideas which is normal among boys and girls of fifteen.
ODELL SHEPHERD, of Louisa May Alcott

[D. H.] Lawrence looked like a plaster gnome on a stone toadstool in some suburban garden.
EDITH SITWELL

Virginia Woolf's writing is no more than glamorous knitting. I believe she must have a pattern.
EDITH SITWELL

He walked as if he had fouled his small clothes and looks as if he smelt it.
CHRISTOPHER SMART, of Thomas Gray

In conversation he is even duller than in writing, if that is possible.
JULIANA SMITH, of Noah Webster

Thomas Carlyle has occasional flashes of silence that make his conversation perfectly delightful.
SYDNEY SMITH

It is written by a man with a diseased mind and soul so black that he would even obscure the darkness of hell.
SENATOR REED SMOOT, of James Joyce's *Ulysses*

A village explainer. Excellent if you were a village, but if you were not, not.
GERTRUDE STEIN, of Ezra Pound

A large shaggy dog, just unchained, scouring the beaches of the world and baying at the moon.
ROBERT LOUIS STEVENSON, of Walt Whitman

He has the most remarkable and seductive genius – and I should say about the smallest in the world.
LYTTON STRACHEY, of Max Beerbohm

The verses, when they were written, resembled nothing so much as spoonfuls of boiling oil, ladled out by a fiendish monkey at an upstairs window upon such of the passers-by whom the wretch had a grudge against.
LYTTON STRACHEY, of Alexander Pope

Then Edith Sitwell appeared, her nose longer than an anteater's, and read some of her absurd stuff.
LYTTON STRACHEY

[Richard] Steele might become a reasonably good writer if he would pay a little attention to grammar, learn something about the propriety and disposition of words and, incidentally, get some information on the subject he intends to handle.

JONATHAN SWIFT

A gap-toothed and hoary ape, who now in his dotage spits and chatters from a dirtier perch of his own finding, and fouling.

ALGERNON CHARLES SWINBURNE, of Ralph Waldo Emerson

He has plenty of music in him, but he cannot get it out.

ALFRED, LORD TENNYSON, of Robert Browning

[Thomas] Carlyle is a poet to whom nature has denied the faculty of verse.

ALFRED, LORD TENNYSON

A louse in the locks of literature.

ALFRED, LORD TENNYSON, of critic Churton Collins

Reading him is like wading through glue.

ALFRED, LORD TENNYSON, of Ben Jonson

Isn't she a poisonous thing of a woman, lying, concealing, flipping, plagiarising, misquoting, and being as clever a crooked literary publicist as ever?

DYLAN THOMAS, of Edith Sitwell

Walt Whitman was not only eager to talk about himself but reluctant to have the conversation stray from the subject for too long.
HENRY D. THOREAU

You talk about yourself a great deal. That's why there are no distinctive characters in your writing. Your characters are all alike. You probably don't understand women; you've never depicted one successfully.
LEO TOLSTOY, to Maxim Gorky

Of [Charles] Dickens's style it is impossible to speak in praise. It is jerky, ungrammatical and created by himself in defiance of rules.
ANTHONY TROLLOPE

To me Edgar Allan Poe's prose is unreadable – like Jane Austen's. No, there's a difference. I could read his prose on a salary, but not Jane's.
MARK TWAIN

Jane Austen's books, too, are absent from this library. Just that one omission alone would make a fairly good library out of a library that hadn't a book in it.
MARK TWAIN

Once you've put one of his books down, you simply can't pick it up again.
MARK TWAIN, of Henry James

George Bernard Shaw: the spinster aunt of English literature.
KENNETH TYNAN

[Truman] Capote's gift for publicity is the most glittering star in his diadem.
GORE VIDAL

It was a good career move.
GORE VIDAL, of Truman Capote's death

What other culture could have produced someone like [Ernest] Hemingway and *not* seen the joke?
GORE VIDAL

Norman Mailer is now what he wanted to be: the patron saint of bad journalism.
GORE VIDAL

An hour with a dentist without Novocaine was like a minute with Carson McCullers.
GORE VIDAL

Do they keep throwing the book at Jeffrey Archer as an act of revenge for his lousy novels?
KEITH WATERHOUSE

To see him [Stephen Spender] fumbling with our rich and delicate English is like seeing a Sèvres vase in the hands of a chimpanzee.
EVELYN WAUGH

Oscar Wilde was over-dressed, pompous, snobbish, sentimental and vain.
EVELYN WAUGH

The more I think you over the more it comes home to me what an unmitigated Middle Victorian ass you were!
H.G. WELLS, of George Bernard Shaw

If he is rewarded according to his desert his name will stink to all generations.
JOHN WESLEY, of Lord Chesterfied

He is the old maid among novelists.
REBECCA WEST, of H.G. Wells

Tell me, when you're alone with Max [Beerbohm], does he take off his face and reveal his mask?
OSCAR WILDE

As a writer he has mastered everything except language; as a novelist he can do everything except tell a story; as an artist he is everything except articulate.
OSCAR WILDE, of George Meredith

He leads his readers to the latrine and locks them in.
OSCAR WILDE, of George Moore

George Moore wrote excellent English until he discovered grammar.
OSCAR WILDE

He hunts down the obvious with the enthusiasm of a short-sighted detective.
OSCAR WILDE, of James Payn

There are two ways of disliking poetry; one way is to dislike it, the other is to read Pope.
OSCAR WILDE

Books of poetry by young writers are usually promissory notes that are never met.
OSCAR WILDE, of W. B. Yeats

Monsieur Zola is determined to show that if he has not genius he can at least be dull.
OSCAR WILDE

I always said little Truman [Capote] had a voice so high it could only be detected by bats.
TENNESSEE WILLIAMS

His style has the desperate jauntiness of an orchestra fiddling away for dear life on a sinking ship.
EDMUND WILSON, of Evelyn Waugh

Fate has not been kind to Mrs Browning. Nobody reads her, nobody discusses her, nobody troubles to put her in her place.
VIRGINIA WOOLF, of Elizabeth Barrett Browning

Pale, marmoreal [T.S.] Eliot was there last week, like a chapped office boy on a high stool, with a cold in his head.
VIRGINIA WOOLF

He is limp and damp and milder than the breath of a cow.
VIRGINIA WOOLF, of E.M. Forster

No one has written worse English than Mr [Thomas] Hardy in some of his novels – cumbrous, stilted, ugly and inexpressive.
VIRGINIA WOOLF

Her mind is a very thin soil, laid an inch or two upon very barren rock.
VIRGINIA WOOLF, of Katherine Mansfield

I don't care for Osbert [Sitwell]'s prose; the rhododendrons grow to such a height in it.
VIRGINIA WOOLF

In the throes of composition George S. Kaufman seems to crawl up the walls of the apartment in the manner of the late Count Dracula.
ALEXANDER WOOLLCOTT

Reading Proust is like bathing in someone else's dirty water.
ALEXANDER WOOLLCOTT

A man carved from a turnip looking out from astonished eyes.
W.B. YEATS, of George Moore

The way Bernard Shaw believes in himself is very refreshing in these atheistic days when so many people believe in no God at all.
ISRAEL ZANGWILL

Media

Newspapers and Magazines

Howard Cosell was gonna be a boxer when he was a kid, only they couldn't find a mouthpiece big enough.
MUHAMMAD ALI

They should give gossip columnist Joyce Haber open-heart surgery – and go in through her feet.
JULIE ANDREWS

Nigel Dempster thinks he has the might of a duke and the gravitas of a senior politician. He believes that if Britain's 200 top men were profiled, he would be among them.
ANON

Take one black widow spider, cross it with a scorpion, wean their poisonous offspring on a mixture of prussic acid and treacle, and you'll get the honeyed sting of Hedda Hopper.
ANON

Drew Pearson can find scandal in Snow White's relations with the Seven Dwarfs.
WILLIAM F. BUCKLEY JR

Gossip columnist Rona Barrett doesn't need a steak knife. She cuts her food with her tongue.
JOHNNY CARSON

No woman of our time has gone further with less mental equipment.
CLIFTON FADIMAN, of Clare Boothe Luce

A low-mouthed, blatant, witless, brutal scoundrel.
HORACE GREELEY, of James Gordon Bennett

A demented bag lady.
ALAN PARKER, of movie critic Pauline Kael

Wherever does he find them?
DOROTHY PARKER, on hearing that Clare Boothe Luce is supposedly kind to her inferiors

No self-respecting fish would want to be wrapped in a [Rupert] Murdoch newspaper.
GEORGE ROYKO

Hedda Hopper is as timid as a buzzsaw.
CASEY SHAWHAN

There is one columnist in Washington who wouldn't have room on his breast if he got a ribbon for every time he's been called a liar.
HARRY S. TRUMAN, of Drew Pearson

A midnight ghoul preying on rottenness and repulsive filth.
WALT WHITMAN, of James Gordon Bennett

Frank Harris is invited to all of the great houses in England
– once.
OSCAR WILDE

The nicest thing I can say about Frances Farmer is that she
is unbearable.
WILLIAM WYLER

Radio and Television

Noel Edmonds has been nominated for a BAFTA. Boy, he
must feel five feet tall.
PAUL ADAMS

The secret of Matthew Kelly's appeal remains a closely
guarded secret.
ANON

Running the marathon is no great hardship compared to the
tortuous ordeal of being interviewed afterwards by Sally
Gunnell.
ANON

Richard Madeley has the looks and personality of a shop-
window dummy.
ANON

Tests have proven that the best way to get your children to go to bed early is to tell them they can stay up and watch Graham Norton.
ANON

Sir Alan Sugar has the looks and charm of a warthog long since ostracised by polite warthog society.
ANON

Noel Edmonds looks just the sort of chap to chip in, "You can tell it's only ketchup," halfway through a horror movie.
CRAIG BROWN

I'm just grateful that Simon Bates is too hideous for TV.
GARRY BUSHELL

Graham Norton puts the flaw in dance floor.
GARRY BUSHELL

Des O'Connor is suffering from a hernia. Is it any wonder? He's been carrying Melanie Sykes for years.
GARRY BUSHELL

A miserable old bat.
ANNA FORD, of Michael Buerk

Newsreader Moira Stuart has the type of face that would look good peering over a five-barred gate.
STAFFORD HILDRED

The man who wears his hair back to front.
FRANKIE HOWERD, of David Frost

John McCririck looks like a hedge dragged through a man backwards.
CLIVE JAMES

Murray [Walker] sounds like a blindfolded man riding a unicycle on the rim of the pit of doom.
CLIVE JAMES

[Terry] Wogan's is a bionic smile if I ever saw one. My guess is that the BBC built him in their own workshops.
CLIVE JAMES

If degrees were handed out for bumptiousness, he would emerge with first-class honours.
JOHN JUNOR, of David Dimbleby

Good taste would likely have the same effect on Howard Stern that daylight has on Dracula.
TED KOPPEL

I never watch the *Dinah Shore Show* – I'm a diabetic.
OSCAR LEVANT

He rose without a trace.
KITTY MUGGERIDGE, of David Frost

A self-styled ogre whose views are as outdated as one of his clunky old computers.
ALLISON PEARSON, of Alan Sugar

[Chris] Evans is caught in some Eighties time warp, as dated as a Sony Walkman in an iPod world.
AMANDA PLATELL

Clearly newsreader Natasha Kaplinsky is to become the acceptable face of BBC dumbing down. They certainly don't come much dumber.
AMANDA PLATELL

In the next episode of Anna Nicole Smith's reality series, she talks about the worst four years of her life. Third grade.
JOAN RIVERS

Is it true that you make your own yoghurt – you get a pint of milk and stare at it?
TED ROBBINS, to Anne Robinson

Diddy David Hamilton has a hair-do which makes him look like a newly thatched cottage.
JEAN ROOK

Top hats look 100 per cent ridiculous on anybody, but on, for example, Willie Carson, it's like attaching a factory chimney to a bungalow.
GILES SMITH

Malcolm Muggeridge: a garden gnome expelled from Eden.
KENNETH TYNAN

A hyena in syrup.
YEVGENY YEVTUSHENKO, of Barbara Walters

Movies

Katharine Hepburn has a cheekbone like a death's head allied to a manner as sinister and aggressive as crossbones.
JAMES AGATE

Surely nobody but a mother could have loved Bette Davis at the height of her career.
BRIAN AHERNE

Charlie Chaplin was a second-rate bicycle-acrobat who should have kept his mouth shut.
KINGSLEY AMIS

Who can forget Mel Gibson in *Hamlet*? Though many have tried.
HARRY ANDREWS

Arnold Schwarzenegger's acting is limited. He has an inability to pick up light objects, such as a telephone, in any sort of naturalistic way.
NIGEL ANDREWS

Gary Cooper had two emotions: "hat on" and "hat off".
ANON

To call Charlton Heston wooden would be to risk a lawsuit from the Forestry Commission.
ANON

Victor Mature sneers and curls his upper lip so often, it gives the impression he had it permanently waved.
ANON

Margaret Rutherford's appearance suggests an overstuffed electric chair. Her writhing stare could reduce a rabid dog to a foaming jelly.
ANON

If you cross agent Ray Stark, you'd better make sure he's dead first.
ANON

The first rule for a young director to follow is not to direct like Michael Winner. The second and third rules are the same.
ANON

Michael Winner's films are atrocious, but they are not the worst thing about him.
ANON

When Al Jolson attends a wedding he wants to be the bride and when he attends a funeral he wants to be the corpse.
LOU ANTHONY

You could never do two films in a row with David Puttnam.
You have to go and bathe your wounds in between.
MICHAEL APTED

Acting is not his forte. Neither is being humble.
ROSANNA ARQUETTE, of Jean-Claude Van Damme

When you talk about a great actor, you're not talking about
Tom Cruise.
LAUREN BACALL

A great artiste, but a small human being.
JOSEPHINE BAKER, of Maurice Chevalier

Katharine Hepburn isn't really stand-offish. She ignores
everyone equally.
LUCILLE BALL

When I get hold of her, I'll tear every hair out of her
moustache!
TALLULAH BANKHEAD, of Bette Davis

Bette Davis and I are good friends. There's nothing I
wouldn't say to her face – both of them.
TALLULAH BANKHEAD

Pola Negri couldn't act her way out of a paper bag.
TALLULAH BANKHEAD

Movies

I suppose Kirk Douglas looks all right if your tastes happen to run to septuagenarians with blow-waves and funny stretch marks round the ears.
LYNN BARBER

Nowadays, Robert Redford's skin looks like a child's sandpit after heavy rain.
LYNN BARBER

If that child had been born in the Middle Ages, she'd have been burned as a witch.
LIONEL BARRYMORE, of Margaret O'Brien

I knew Elizabeth Taylor when she didn't know where her next husband was coming from.
ANNE BAXTER

She has a face that belongs to the sea and the wind, with large rocking-horse nostrils and teeth that you just know bite an apple every day.
CECIL BEATON, of Katharine Hepburn

A broad with a big future behind her.
CONSTANCE BENNETT, of Marilyn Monroe

I'm a little repulsed by her shining lips, like balloon tyres in wet weather.
JOHN BETJEMAN, of Joan Crawford

One wishes that Julie Andrews didn't always give the impression that she had just left her horse in the hallway.
MICHAEL BILLINGTON

Renée Zellweger looks like a painted pumpkin on a pogo stick.
MR BLACKWELL

Working with Cher was like being in a blender with an alligator.
PETER BOGDANOVICH

He seems to think he's Lee Marvin – except he's two feet shorter and about one third the talent.
JOHN BOORMAN, of Mel Gibson

Peter Sellers was his own worst enemy although there was lots of competition.
ROY BOULTING

Mr [James] Dean appears to be wearing my last year's wardrobe and using my last year's talent.
MARLON BRANDO

He's the kind of guy that when he dies, he's going to go to heaven and give God a bad time for making him bald.
MARLON BRANDO, of Frank Sinatra

Maggie Smith used to have excellent skin but in a few more years they'll have to unfold it to find out who she used to be.
JEREMY BRETT

Wet she's a star, dry she ain't.
FANNY BRICE, of Esther Williams

Steve McQueen's features resembled a fossilised wash rag.
ALAN BRIEN

Evelyn [Brent]'s idea of acting was to march into a scene, spread her legs and stand flat-footed and read her lines with masculine defiance.
LOUISE BROOKS

Mel Tolkin looks like a stork that dropped a baby and broke it and is coming to explain to the parents.
MEL BROOKS

Cecil B. DeMille was De phoney and De hypocrite of all time.
YUL BRYNNER

She has an insipid double chin, her legs are too short, and she has a slight potbelly.
RICHARD BURTON, of Elizabeth Taylor

He has a face like two profiles stuck together.
MRS PATRICK CAMPBELL, of Basil Rathbone

Tallulah [Bankhead] is always skating on thin ice, and everyone wants to be there when it breaks.
MRS PATRICK CAMPBELL

Watching the non-dancing, non-singing Fred Astaire is like watching a grounded skylark.
VINCENT CANBY

I don't think he could direct his nephew to the bathroom.
DYAN CANNON, of Otto Preminger

Dry and draughty, like an abandoned temple.
TRUMAN CAPOTE, of Greta Garbo

Life is difficult enough without Meryl Streep movies. And she looks like a chicken.
TRUMAN CAPOTE

Ricardo Montalban is to improvised acting what Mount Rushmore is to animation.
JOHN CASSAVETES

He has no sense of humour, particularly about himself.
LITA GREY CHAPLIN, of Charlie Chaplin

[Humphrey] Bogart's a helluva nice guy until 11.30 pm. After that he thinks he's Bogart.
DAVE CHASEN

Jamie Lee Curtis has trouble learning her lines because English is not her first language. She doesn't, unfortunately, have a first language.
JOHN CLEESE

Last month Catherine Zeta Jones raised a few eyebrows with her flirty behaviour with veteran actor Sean Connery, a man old enough to be her husband.
MARTIN CLUNES

I'd wring your neck, if you had one.
NOËL COWARD, to Claudette Colbert

If you'd been any prettier it would have been *Florence of Arabia*.
NOËL COWARD, to Peter O'Toole

I don't see how she built a career out of a set of mannerisms instead of acting ability. Take away the pop eyes, the cigarette and those funny clipped words, and what have you got? She's a phoney.
JOAN CRAWFORD, of Bette Davis

I didn't know Judy Garland well, but after watching her in action I didn't want to.
JOAN CRAWFORD

A spoiled, indulgent child, a blemish on public decency.
JOAN CRAWFORD, of Elizabeth Taylor

Towards the end of her life she looked like a hungry insect magnified a million times – a praying mantis that had forgotten how to pray.
QUENTIN CRISP, of Joan Crawford

There's nothing I wouldn't do for Bob [Hope], and there's nothing he wouldn't do for me. And that's the way we go through life – doing nothing for each other.
BING CROSBY

Louis B. Meyer's arm around your shoulder meant his hand was closer to your throat.
JULES DASSIN

His big asset: a face that would look well upon a three-toed sloth.
RUSSELL DAVIES, of Sylvester Stallone

Keanu Reeves? I couldn't cast someone who sounds like a small Polynesian island.
TERENCE DAVIES

She was divinely, hysterically, insanely malevolent.
BETTE DAVIS, of Theda Bara

Her face was her talent, and when it dropped, so did her career, right out of sight.
BETTE DAVIS, of Constance Bennett

Why am I so good at playing bitches? I think it's because I'm not a bitch. Maybe that's why Miss [Joan] Crawford always plays ladies.
BETTE DAVIS

The best time I ever had with Joan Crawford was when I pushed her down the stairs in *Whatever Happened to Baby Jane?*
BETTE DAVIS

Those eyebrows wound up looking like African caterpillars.
BETTE DAVIS, of Joan Crawford

Joan [Crawford] always cries a lot. Her tear ducts must be close to her bladder.
BETTE DAVIS

Lillian Gish ought to know about close-ups. Jesus, she was around when they invented them!
BETTE DAVIS

I always admire Katharine Hepburn's cheekbones – more than her films.
BETTE DAVIS

She sounds more and more like Donald Duck.
BETTE DAVIS, of Katharine Hepburn

Dramatic art, in her opinion, is knowing how to fill a sweater.
BETTE DAVIS, of Jayne Mansfield

In his bodybuilding days Arnold Schwarzenegger was known as the Austrian Oak. Then he started acting and was known as . . . the Austrian Oak.
JACK DEE

She has a face to launch a thousand dredgers.
JACK DE MANIO, of Glenda Jackson

He has eyes like a weasel.
SANDY DENNIS, of Alec Baldwin

Poor Elsa [Lanchester]. She left England because it already had a queen – Victoria. And she wanted to be queen of the Charles Laughton household once he became a star, but he already had the role.
MARLENE DIETRICH

I acted vulgar. Madonna *is* vulgar.
MARLENE DIETRICH

A day away from Tallulah [Bankhead] is like a month in the country.
HOWARD DIETZ

Mickey Rooney's favourite exercise is climbing tall people.
PHYLLIS DILLER

It's probably her greatest performance ever because she's playing a chef – and she can't boil water!
MICHAEL DOUGLAS, of wife Catherine Zeta Jones

A self-important, boring, flash-in-the-pan Brit.
ROBERT DOWNEY JR, of Hugh Grant

Zsa Zsa Gabor had three or four operations on her nose and it got worse every time. It looks like an electric plug that you put in a wall.
ANITA EKBERG

In order to feel safe on his private jet, John Travolta has purchased a bomb-sniffing dog. Unfortunately for the actor, the dog came six movies too late.
JIMMY FALLON

He was an aloof, remote person, intent on being Cary Grant playing Cary Grant playing Cary Grant.
FRANCES FARMER

I wouldn't want to be a dog, a horse, or a woman around Howard Hawks.
WILLIAM FAULKNER

A plumber's idea of Cleopatra.
W.C. FIELDS, of Mae West

Debbie Reynolds was indeed the girl next door. But only if you lived next door to a self-centred, totally driven, insecure, untruthful phoney.
EDDIE FISHER

Acting with [Laurence] Harvey is like acting by yourself – only worse.
JANE FONDA

Secretly, I think Bob is afraid of women. He likes to tell them what to do. He likes them to be subservient. He treated me as if I were an extra or something.
JANE FONDA, of Robert Redford

Joan Crawford had perfect posture, but it was rather intimidating. She looked as if she'd swallowed a yardstick.
GLENN FORD

There are two things I would never do – climb Mount Everest and work with Val Kilmer again.
JOHN FRANKENHEIMER

Today you see Julia Roberts and Cameron Diaz running around looking unkempt in jogging trousers, they look like bag ladies, like homeless people.
VALENTINO GARAVINI

Clark Gable is the kind of guy who, if you say, "Hiya, Clark, how are you?", is stuck for an answer.
AVA GARDNER

When Frank Sinatra was down he was sweet, but when he got back up he was hell.
AVA GARDNER

Frank [Sinatra] and I were always great in bed. The trouble usually started on the way to the bidet.
AVA GARDNER

I always knew Frank would end up in bed with a boy.
AVA GARDNER, of Frank Sinatra's marriage to Mia Farrow

My daughter [Liza Minnelli] has got a voice like chalk on a blackboard.
JUDY GARLAND

Lana Turner's a nice girl, but it's like sitting in a room with a beautiful vase.
JUDY GARLAND

I don't know his name but he's got a face like half a teapot.
KING GEORGE VI, of Ralph Richardson

Dear Ingrid [Bergman]. Speaks five languages and can't act in any of them.
JOHN GIELGUD

The only thing worse than not being nominated for an Oscar would have been to be nominated and then losing to Cher. That would have been embarrassing.
LILLIAN GISH

The only reason so many people showed up at his funeral was because they wanted to make sure he was dead.
SAM GOLDWYN, of Louis B. Meyer

It took longer to make one of Mary Pickford's contracts than it did to make one of Mary's pictures.
SAM GOLDWYN

There have been times when I've been ashamed to take the money. But then I think of some of the movies that have given [Laurence] Olivier cash for his old age, and I don't feel so bad.
STEWART GRANGER

Ken Russell is an arrogant, self-centred, petulant individual.
BOB GUCCIONE

Julie Andrews is like a nun with a switchblade.
LESLIE HALLIWELL

A man of many talents, all of them minor.
LESLIE HALLIWELL, of Blake Edwards

Oliver Stone is a heavy-handed propagandist, and the women in his films make Barbie look like Sylvia Plath.
JANE HAMSHER

You're doing it the wrong way round, my boy. You're a star and you don't know how to act.
SIR CEDRIC HARDWICKE, to Richard Chamberlain

An over-fat, flatulent, sixty-two-year-old windbag, a master of inconsequence now masquerading as a guru, passing off his vast limitations as pious virtues.
RICHARD HARRIS, of Michael Caine

If you were more of a woman, I would be more of a man. Kissing you is like kissing the side of a beer bottle.
LAURENCE HARVEY, to Capucine

The source of Woody Allen's popularity has always escaped me; I find him a very thin slice of Harold Lloyd on rye.
ROBERT HATCH

I learned an awful lot from him by doing exactly the opposite.
HOWARD HAWKS, of Cecil B. DeMille

There is not enough money in Hollywood to lure me into making another film with Joan Crawford.
STERLING HAYDEN

Goldie Hawn has the general squeaky-voiced persona of a vaguely disturbed chipmunk.
SUE HEAL

Firing people came as naturally as breathing to Harry Cohn, more naturally in fact.
BEN HECHT

Movies

Tallulah [Bankhead] was sitting in a group of people, giving the monologue she always thought was conversation.
LILLIAN HELLMAN

A face unclouded by thought.
LILLIAN HELLMAN, of Norma Shearer

Any picture in which Errol Flynn is the best actor is its own worst enemy.
ERNEST HEMINGWAY

Isn't it wonderful you've had such a great career when you had no right to have a career at all?
KATHARINE HEPBURN, to Dorothy Arzner

You can't direct a [Charles] Laughton picture. The best you can hope for is to referee.
ALFRED HITCHCOCK

Pierce Brosnan always reminds me of the models in men's knitwear catalogues.
PAUL HOGGART

Richard E. Grant always plays the same basic character, simply varying the degree of intensity with which he rolls his eyeballs.
PAUL HOGGART

Billy Wilder has a mind full of razor blades.
WILLIAM HOLDEN

You can calculate Zsa Zsa Gabor's age by the rings on her fingers.
BOB HOPE

You had to stand in line to hate him.
HEDDA HOPPER, of Harry Cohn

I did not give Lee Majors his start in acting – you can't pin that one on me.
ROCK HUDSON

Clark Gable's ears make him look like a taxicab with both doors open.
HOWARD HUGHES

There have always been mixed opinions about Charles Bronson. Some people hate him like poison and some people just hate him regular.
JILL IRELAND

Marilyn Monroe was so minimally gifted as to be almost unemployable.
CLIVE JAMES

I can't see what Jack L. Warner can do with an Oscar – it can't say yes.
AL JOLSON

Glamour is what Julie Andrews doesn't have. She does her duties efficiently but mechanically, like an airline stewardess.
PAULINE KAEL

Cecil B. DeMille made small-minded pictures on a big scale.
PAULINE KAEL

Robert Redford has turned almost alarmingly blond – he's gone past platinum, he must be plutonium; his hair is co-ordinated with his teeth.
PAULINE KAEL

To know him was to like him. Not to know him was to love him.
BERT KALMAR, of Herman Mankiewicz

Harry Cohn liked to be the biggest bug in the manure pile.
ELIA KAZAN

A great actress, from the waist down.
MARGARET KENDAL, of Sarah Bernhardt

Boiled down to essentials, she [Greta Garbo] is a plain mortal girl with large feet.
HERBERT KRETZMER

Sam Peckinpah is like an old dog you sometimes have to apologise for.
KRIS KRISTOFFERSON

Working with Barbra Streisand is pretty stressful. It's like sitting down to a picnic in the middle of a freeway.
KRIS KRISTOFFERSON

Filming with Streisand is an experience which may have cured me of movies.
KRIS KRISTOFFERSON

Underneath his aggressive, gruff exterior is pure Brillo.
HARRY KURNITZ, of Billy Wilder

Bill [W. C. Fields] never really wanted to hurt anybody. He just felt an obligation.
GREGORY LA CAVA

I can safely say that I don't have any interest in Lindsay Lohan – nor do I understand anyone else that does.
NICK LACHEY

Kirk [Douglas] would be the first to tell you that he's a difficult man; I would be the second.
BURT LANCASTER

She looked as though butter wouldn't melt in her mouth – or anywhere else for that matter.
ELSA LANCHESTER, of Maureen O'Hara

She's better on stage, from a distance. On a screen, close up, she makes you want to dive for cover.
ELSA LANCHESTER, of Maggie Smith

I think it's so quaint that she's making a whole new career out of merely being very old. But I hope I never live so long that I get hired simply for not being a corpse!
ELSA LANCHESTER, of Estelle Winwood

Ava Gardner was her customary self, as amiable as an adder.
HELEN LAWRENSON

George Hamilton is audibly tan.
FRAN LEBOWITZ

An inveterate liar who lived in a fantasy world.
KELLY LEBROCK, of Steven Seagal

For some people, Bela Lugosi was the embodiment of dark, mysterious forces, a harbinger of evil from the world of shadow. For others he was merely a ham actor appearing in a type of film unsuitable for children and often unfit for adults.
ARTHUR LENNIG

Michael Caine can out-act any, well nearly any, telephone kiosk you care to mention.
HUGH LEONARD

Don't forget it's daylight saving time. You spring forward, then you fall back. It's like Robert Downey Jr getting out of bed.
DAVID LETTERMAN

Joan Crawford should have puppies, not children.
OSCAR LEVANT

The only person who left the Iron Curtain wearing it.
OSCAR LEVANT, of Zsa Zsa Gabor

Zsa Zsa Gabor has discovered the secret of perpetual middle age.
OSCAR LEVANT

Judy Garland: a vibrato in search of a voice.
OSCAR LEVANT

Laurence Olivier is the most overrated actor on earth. Take away the wives and the looks, and you have John Gielgud.
OSCAR LEVANT

Al Jolson's ego was such that when he heard applause for another star, he reacted as though he had been robbed.
HENRY LEVIN

Chuck Norris is an actor whose lack of expression is so profound that it could be mistaken for icily controlled technique.
NICHOLAS LEZARD

Sophia Loren plays peasants. I play ladies.
GINO LOLLOBRIGIDA

Clara [Bow] was the idol of the illiterate, and from her dainty lips came nothing more seductive than bubble gum.
ANITA LOOS

Her favourite form of exercise was walking off a movie set.
ANITA LOOS, of Louise Brooks

Jack Nicholson is a legend in his own lifetime and in his own mind.
JENNIFER LOPEZ

In Hollywood she's revered, she gets nominated for Oscars, but I've never heard anyone in the public or among my friends say, "Oh, I love Winona Ryder."
JENNIFER LOPEZ

Her personality is limited. She is good as a peasant but incapable of playing a lady.
SOPHIA LOREN, of Gina Lollobrigida

Whatever Francis [Ford Coppola] does for you always ends up benefiting Francis most.
GEORGE LUCAS

A mean, tipsy, powerful, rotten-egg lady.
MERCEDES MCCAMBRIDGE, of Joan Crawford

Doris Day is as wholesome as a bowl of cornflakes and at least as sexy.
DWIGHT MACDONALD

Joseph Losey is a versatile director who commands a wide range of styles for wrecking a movie.
DWIGHT MACDONALD

His life was a fifty-year trespass against good taste.
LESLIE MALLORY, of Errol Flynn

He has the memory of an elephant and the hide of an elephant. The only difference is that elephants are vegetarians and Mayer's diet is his fellow man.
HERMAN J. MANKIEWICZ, of Louis B. Mayer

Lana Turner could give you an eyewitness account of the Crucifixion and still put you to sleep.
HERMAN J. MANKIEWICZ

If Mel Brooks had come up in my time he wouldn't have qualified to be a busboy.
JOSEPH L. MANKIEWICZ

The once-beautiful, most distinguished actor of our time has turned into a self-loathing slob and left a lot of human wreckage in his wake.
PETER MANSO, of Marlon Brando

Co-starring with [Greta] Garbo hardly constituted an introduction.
FREDRIC MARCH

Hollywood is full of pale imitations of Pamela Anderson and, worse still, Pamela Anderson herself.
LISA MARCHANT

After Arnold Schwarzenegger, Dolph Lundgren is a bit of a disappointment. At least Arnold looks as if he comes supplied with batteries.
ADAM MARS-JONES

The oars aren't touching the water these days.
DEAN MARTIN, of Shirley MacLaine

There's a statue of Jimmy Stewart in the Hollywood Wax Museum, and the statue talks better than he does.
DEAN MARTIN

Movies

Now there sits a man with an open mind. You can feel the draught from here.
GROUCHO MARX, of Chico Marx

The only man who could throw a seven with one die.
HARPO MARX, of Sam Goldwyn

Dudley Moore has a club foot. That's not a problem – for him, his career, or anyone. What I object to is his club wit.
JAMES MASON

I've met a lot of hard-boiled eggs in my time, but you – you're twenty minutes!
WALTER MATTHAU, to Barbra Streisand

I'd love to work with Barbra Streisand again. In something appropriate. Perhaps *Macbeth*.
WALTER MATTHAU

Farrah Fawcett is uniquely suited to play a woman of limited intelligence.
MICHAEL MEDVED

Raquel Welch is one of the few actresses in Hollywood history who looks more animated in still photographs than she does on the screen.
MICHAEL MEDVED

I remember my brother once saying, "I'd like to marry Elizabeth Taylor," and my father said, "Don't worry, your time will come."
SPIKE MILLIGAN

63

Mother was the real-life Wicked Witch of the West.
LIZA MINNELLI, of Judy Garland

I gave up being serious about making pictures about the time I made a film with Greer Garson and she took 127 takes to say "no".
ROBERT MITCHUM

I once heard a producer say about Howard Hughes: "He's entitled to his own opinion – and as many others as money can buy."
ROBERT MITCHUM

A Steve McQueen performance lends itself to monotony.
ROBERT MITCHUM

Burt Lancaster couldn't pick up an ashtray before discussing his motivation for an hour or so.
JEANNE MOREAU

To the unwashed public, Joan Collins is a star. But to those who know her, she's a commodity who would sell her own bowel movement.
ANTHONY NEWLEY

You knew where you were with Errol [Flynn] – he always let you down.
DAVID NIVEN

Miss United Dairies herself.
DAVID NIVEN, of Jayne Mansfield

George Sanders had a face, even in his twenties, which looked as though he had rented it on a long lease and had lived in it for so long he didn't want to move out.
DAVID NIVEN

She [Loretta Young] was doing a scene, urging Richard the Lionheart to go to the Middle East and fight. Loretta read her line, "Richard, you gotta save Christianity", but not very convincingly. So DeMille took her aside and asked her to put some awe into her line reading. They re-shot the scene and she said: "Aw, Richard, you gotta save Christianity!"
DAVID NIVEN

Sean Connery has such a deep love of Scotland that he refuses to use anything other than a Scottish accent no matter what role he is taking.
GRAHAM NORTON

She wasn't very good. She was fine when she was six or seven. But did you notice how she couldn't act when she was fourteen?
TATUM O'NEAL, of Shirley Temple

There are three types of actress: the silly, the very silly, and Shirley MacLaine.
P.J. O'ROURKE

Quentin Tarantino has the vocal modulation of a railway station announcer, the expressive power of a fence-post and the charisma of a week-old head of lettuce.
FINTAN O'TOOLE

65

Marion Davies has two expressions: joy and indigestion.
DOROTHY PARKER

She ran the gamut of emotions from A to B.
DOROTHY PARKER, of Katharine Hepburn

Joan Collins looks like she combs her hair with an egg-beater.
LOUELLA PARSONS

Working for the Marx Brothers was not unlike being chained to a galley car and lashed at ten-minute intervals.
S.J. PERELMAN

I'd rather have a cannibal for a co-star.
ANTHONY PERKINS, of Joan Crawford

Where some men are self-contained, he's vacuum-packed!
ANTHONY PERKINS, of Steven Seagal

Barbra Streisand: the most pretentious woman the cinema has ever known.
JON PETERS

The sensitivity of a starving elephant.
FRANK PIERSON, of Barbra Streisand

Working with Julie Andrews is like being hit over the head by a Valentine's Day card.
CHRISTOPHER PLUMMER

Agent Mike Ovitz is even colder than his air-conditioned office.
JULIA PHILLIPS

Johnny Depp puts the dire in director.
EDWARD PORTER

Directing Marilyn Monroe was like directing Lassie. You needed fourteen takes to get each one of them right.
OTTO PREMINGER

A vacuum with nipples.
OTTO PREMINGER, of Marilyn Monroe

To read Shirley MacLaine's autobiography is to encounter one of the most inflated airheads ever to break free of her moorings.
JOHN PRESTON

As a human being, Joan Crawford is a very great actress.
NICHOLAS RAY

Jean Harlow was not a good actress, not even by Hollywood standards.
WILLIAM REDFIELD

Paul Newman has the attention span of a lightning bolt.
ROBERT REDFORD

Working with Glenda Jackson was like being run over by a Bedford truck.
OLIVER REED

Interviewing Warren Beatty is like asking a haemophiliac for a pint of blood.
REX REED

Most of the time he sounds like he has a mouth full of toilet paper.
REX REED, of Marlon Brando

He is to acting what Liberace was to pumping iron.
REX REED, of Sylvester Stallone

I can sing as well as Fred Astaire can act.
BURT REYNOLDS

He has preserved the mentality of an adolescent. When he doesn't try and someone's speaking to him, it's like a blank wall. In fact it's even less interesting because behind a blank wall you can always suppose that there's something interesting there.
BURT REYNOLDS, of Marlon Brando

If Kathleen Turner had been a man, I would have punched her out long ago.
BURT REYNOLDS

In future, Kevin Costner should only appear in pictures that he directs himself. That way he can always be working with his favourite actor and his favourite director.
KEVIN REYNOLDS

Make yourself at home, Frank. Hit somebody.
DON RICKLES, to Frank Sinatra

In the new movie *Paycheck*, Ben Affleck plays a man who loses two years of his memory. Let's hope it's the two years he was making *Pearl Harbor*.
JOAN RIVERS

Bo Derek does not understand the concept of Roman numerals. She thought we fought in World War Eleven.
JOAN RIVERS

The DVD of Mariah Carey's movie *Glitter* is coming out with bonus features. Maybe one of them will be a plot.
JOAN RIVERS

Jane Fonda didn't get that terrific body from exercise. She got it from lifting all that money.
JOAN RIVERS

Melanie Griffith is very sweet but dumb – the lights are on but the dogs aren't barking.
JOAN RIVERS

I saw Angelina Jolie on TV. Those lips are so big, she could whisper in her own ear.
JOAN RIVERS

Is Elizabeth Taylor fat? Her favourite food is seconds.
JOAN RIVERS

Everyone is going on about how great Julia [Roberts] was in *Erin Brokovich*, but what did she actually do? Wear push-up bras. It wasn't great acting.
ERIC ROBERTS

Gwyneth Paltrow is quite pretty in a British, horsey sort of way.
JULIA ROBERTS

Cedric Hardwicke had the personality and drive of an old tortoise hunting for lettuce.
RACHEL ROBERTS

Jean-Claude Van Damme exudes the charisma of a packet of Cup-A-Soup.
JONATHAN ROMNEY

I've staged shows that called for the management of a herd of buffalo, and I've shot actors out of cannons for fifty feet into the arms of an adagio dancer, but both of them were easier than saying "Good morning" to Tallulah Bankhead.
BILLY ROSE

Richard E. Grant looks rather like one of those balloons you get from the National Gallery of Munch's *The Scream*, after it's burst.
DEBORAH ROSS

The softest thing about him is his front teeth.
DAMON RUNYON, of Harry Cohn

Bernardo Bertolucci is more of a gangster than a movie director.
MARIA SCHNEIDER

Bette Davis got most of her exercise by putting her foot down.
TOM SHALES

David O. Selznick stormed through life demanding to see
the manager.
LLOYD SHEARER

Jack Lemmon has a gift for butchering good parts while
managing to look intelligent, thus constituting Hollywood's abiding answer to the theatre.
WILFRID SHEED

I've got three words for him: Am A. Teur.
CHARLIE SHEEN, of Colin Farrell

Men find it tougher to adjust to success gracefully. They
throw their weight around and try and make everyone else
feel less than successful. Bruce Willis, for instance . . .
CYBILL SHEPHERD

They say Tom Mix rides as if he's part of the horse, but
they don't say which part.
ROBERT SHERWOOD

Charles Bronson's popularity within the movie industry is
not legendary.
DAVID SHIPMAN

He never bore a grudge against anyone he wronged.
SIMONE SIGNORET, of Jack L. Warner

Robert Altman has most of the qualifications for a major
director except the supreme one of having something
significant to say.
JOHN SIMON

The only real talent Miss [Doris] Day possesses is that of being absolutely sanitary: her personality untouched by human emotions, her brow unclouded by human thought, her form unsmudged by the slightest evidence of femininity.
JOHN SIMON

The insufferably smug and woodchuck-cheeked Minnie Driver proffers what the French call a *tête à gifler* – a face begging to be slapped.
JOHN SIMON

Miss [Judy] Garland's figure resembles the giant economy-size tube of toothpaste in girls' bedrooms. Squeezed intemperately at all points, it acquires a shape that defies definition by the most resourceful solid geometrician.
JOHN SIMON

Since Jean-Luc Godard's films have nothing to say, we could perhaps have ninety minutes of silence instead of each of them.
JOHN SIMON

She has the look of an asexual harlequin.
JOHN SIMON, of Glenda Jackson

You have to have a stomach for ugliness to endure Carol Kane – to say nothing of the zombie-like expressions she mistakes for acting.
JOHN SIMON

He looked like a half-melted rubber bulldog.
JOHN SIMON, of Walter Matthau

Her blackly mascaraed eye-sockets gape like twin craters, unfortunately extinct.
JOHN SIMON, of Melina Mercouri

I always thought Liza Minnelli's face deserving of first prize in a beagle category.
JOHN SIMON

Barbra Streisand: a cross between an aardvark and an albino rat.
JOHN SIMON

Were she to collide with a Mack truck, it is the truck that would drop dead.
JOHN SIMON, of Barbra Streisand

The sad thing is that he has consistently put his very real talents to the task of glorifying his imaginary genius.
JOHN SIMON, of Orson Welles

I'll never put Tom Cruise down. He's already kinda short.
DON SIMPSON

Well, at least he has finally found his true love – what a pity he can't marry himself.
FRANK SINATRA, of Robert Redford

John Frankenheimer went from boy-wonder to has-been without ever passing through the stage of maturity.
NEIL SINYARD

It proves what they always say: give the public what they want to see, and they'll come out for it.
RED SKELTON, on the crowds at Harry Cohn's funeral

Glenn Close is not an actress – she's an address.
MAGGIE SMITH

Kathleen Turner's OK in stills. When she talks and moves about, she reminds me of someone who works in a super-market.
ANN SOTHERN

George Lucas reminded me a little of Walt Disney's version of a mad scientist.
STEVEN SPIELBERG

An appalling man and, even more unforgivably, an appalling actor.
ROBERT STEPHENS, of Laurence Harvey

She lives in rarefied air that's a little thin. It's like she's not getting quite enough oxygen.
SHARON STONE, of Gwyneth Paltrow

Overweight, overbosomed, overpaid, and undertalented.
DAVID SUSKIND, of Elizabeth Taylor

Peter O'Toole had a face not so much lived in as infested.
PAUL TAYLOR

There are times when Richard Gere has the warm effect of a wind tunnel at dawn.
DAVID THOMPSON

Elizabeth Taylor isn't spoiled. I have often seen her pour her own champagne for breakfast.
MIKE TODD

To say she acts would be to overstretch the truth.
CHRISTOPHER TOOKEY, of Kelly Brook

The only hope of this guy ever making a funny movie is for him to switch brains with someone who's actually talented.
CHRISTOPHER TOOKEY, of Rob Schneider

I thank God that neither I nor any member of my family will ever be so hard up that we have to work for Otto Preminger.
LANA TURNER

He is his own worst enemy. If he directs a little romance, it has to be the biggest, most overdone little romance in movie history.
KENNETH TURAN, of Francis Ford Coppola

The four-foot Pole you wouldn't want to touch with a ten-foot pole.
KENNETH TYNAN, of Roman Polanski

Joan Crawford would have made an exemplary prison matron . . . She had the requisite sadism, paranoia and taste for violence.
HARRIET VAN HORNE

He got a reputation as a great actor by just thinking hard about the next line.
KING VIDOR, of Gary Cooper

The only way I could force myself into kissing [Bette] Midler on-camera was to pretend that I was kissing my dog.
KEN WAHL

In one scene in *Jinxed* I have to hit her [Bette Midler] in the face and I thought, we could save some money on sound effects here.
KEN WAHL

Anita Louise: as cold as a stepmother's kiss.
HAL WALLIS

In some of his last movies, Errol Flynn had to play himself. Unfortunately the role was beyond his acting abilities.
JACK L. WARNER

They say Louis B. Mayer is his own worst enemy. Not while I'm still alive.
JACK L. WARNER

When it comes to men, I heard she never turns anything down except the bedcovers.
MAE WEST, of Jayne Mansfield

When he found a voice to say what was on his mind, he was like a child of eight writing lyrics for Beethoven's Ninth.
BILLY WILDER, of Charlie Chaplin

She has breasts like granite and a brain like Swiss cheese, full of holes.
BILLY WILDER, of Marilyn Monroe

I am the only director who ever made two pictures with Marilyn Monroe. Forget the Oscar, I deserve the Purple Heart.
BILLY WILDER

What do you mean, heart attack? You've got to have a heart before you can have an attack.
BILLY WILDER, of Peter Sellers

An extremely mean and deeply heartless figure.
PETER WILLES, of David Niven

Lana Turner couldn't act her way out of her form-fitting cashmeres.
TENNESSEE WILLIAMS

Guys like him and [Michael] Caine talk about acting as if they knew what it was.
NICOL WILLIAMSON, of Sean Connery

Tallulah [Bankhead] talked so ceaselessly that you had to make a reservation five minutes ahead to get a word in.
EARL WILSON

Paul Henreid looks as though his idea of fun would be to find a nice cold damp grave and sit in it.
RICHARD WINNINGTON

They'd have to pay me an awful lot of money to work with James Cameron again.
KATE WINSLET

At the RKO studios Hepburn was called "Katharine of Arrogance". Not without reason . . .
ESTELLE WINWOOD

Mamie Van Doren often acted like Mr Ed the Talking Horse.
PAULA YATES

Zsa Zsa Gabor has been married so many times she has rice marks on her face.
HENNY YOUNGMAN

Goldie Hawn was landed with an idiot giggle, a remorseless inclination to squeak and if a brain hummed behind those dumbfounded eyes the secret never leaked out.
DONALD ZEC

Rudolph Valentino's acting is largely confined to protruding his large, almost occult eyes until the vast areas of white are visible, drawing back the lips of his wide, sensuous mouth to bare his gleaming teeth, and flaring his nostrils.
ADOLPH ZUKOR

Biting Reviews

There is enough Irish comedy to make me wish Cromwell had done a more thorough job.
JAMES AGATE, of *Fort Apache*

Several tons of dynamite are set off in this picture – none of it under the right people.
JAMES AGEE, of *Tycoon*

To go or not to go, strewth, that is the question.
ANON, of Mel Gibson's *Hamlet*

Divorce His, Divorce Hers: all the joy of standing by at an autopsy.
ANON

Angela Lansbury wears the crown of France as though she had won it at a county fair.
ANON, of *The Three Musketeers*

Putting on a sad show, courtesy of Liza with a zzzzz.
ANON, of *Stepping Out*, starring Liza Minnelli

David Niven rallying his hardy Highlanders to his standard in a voice hardly large enough to summon a waiter.
ANON, of *Bonnie Prince Charlie*

A million monkeys with a million crayons would be hard-pressed in a million years to create anything as cretinous.
ANON, of *Battlefield Earth*

The kind of picture actors do when they need work.
LEW AYRES, of *Fingers at the Window*

If this film were any more of a dog, it would shed.
JOHN BARBOUR, of *At Long Last Love*

A film so dire it deserves to be reviewed in the obituary column.
LAURA BAUM, of *Heaven's Gate*

As a pompous middle-European intellectual, Kenneth Mars mugs and drools in a manner that Jerry Lewis might find excessive.
JAY COCKS, of *What's Up, Doc?*

Sitting through two hours and twenty minutes is at times like running through treacle wearing flippers.
PETER COX, of *Hook*

All agony, no ecstasy.
JUDITH CRIST, of *The Agony and the Ecstasy*

For once [Robert] Mitchum seems to have an excuse for keeping his eyes at half-mast.
JUDITH CRIST, of *The Man in the Middle*

It's a truly awful book. What an achievement to make a film that is even worse.
DAILY MAIL, of *The Da Vinci Code*

Duets does for karaoke bars what *Jaws* did for the ocean. It features five actors and Huey Lewis. And the News? Not so good.
FRANK DeCARO

Resurrection Man leaves you with the feeling of having been on an occasionally unguided tour of an abattoir.
RICHARD FALCON

The only terrifying thing about *Creepshow 2* is the thought of *Creepshow 3*.
NIGEL FLOYD

In *Titanic*, James Cameron had to invent a Romeo-and-Juliet-style fictional couple to heat up what was a real-life catastrophe. This seems a tiny bit like giving Anne Frank a wacky best friend to perk up the attic.
LIBBY GELMAN-WAXNER

The Incredible Sarah is a job lot of obligatory Hollywood platitudes strung together with all the skill of Captain Hook trying to thread a needle.
BENNY GREEN

The first film to be upstaged by its own credit titles.
BENNY GREEN, of *The Return of the Pink Panther*

The characters speak as if they were dictating important letters.
A.P. HERBERT, of *The Terror*

This is the movie of the book they said could never be filmed. They were right.
TOM HUTCHINSON, of *Naked Lunch*

Cleopatra was the biggest asp disaster in the world.
PAULINE KAEL

An overblown version with songs where they are not needed (and Leslie Bricusse's songs are never needed).
PAULINE KAEL, of *Goodbye Mr Chips*

Famous Put-Downs

The Sound of Mucus.
PAULINE KAEL, of *The Sound of Music*

Not one moment of the picture is anything but garbage under the gravy of false honesty.
STANLEY KAUFFMANN, of *The Way We Were*

Van Johnson does his best: appears.
CAROLINE A. LEJEUNE, of an unnamed film

The visual effect of Draco in *Dragonheart* was achieved using the same technology as that used for *Jurassic Park*, wherein hundreds of supercomputers and thousands of man-hours are used to make the visual effects look every bit as realistic as 1920s bendable clay puppet technology.
MIKE NELSON

[Fredric] March came in like a lion and went out like a ham.
Frank Nugent, of *The Buccaneer*

Sidney Lumet ensures a smooth ride, but as usual takes too long to say what he means and brings the Express in twenty minutes late.
CHRIS PEACHMENT, of *Murder on the Orient Express*

The Hindenburg manages to make one of the century's most sensational real-life catastrophes seem roughly as terrifying as a stubbed toe.
FRANK RICH

Movies

Sheldon Lettich directs with the limpness you associate with the vegetable he's nearly named after.
JONATHAN ROMNEY, of *Double Impact*

Another Woman is a feel-good movie only in the sense that you feel much better when you stop watching it.
SIMON ROSE

Director Gene Wilder has bitten off more than he can chew, and I can swallow.
JOHN SIMON, of *The Adventures of Sherlock Holmes' Smarter Brother*

This film is the platonic idea of boredom, roughly comparable to reading a three-volume novel in a language of which one knows only the alphabet.
John Simon, of *Camelot*

David Lean's *Dr Zhivago* does for snow what his *Lawrence of Arabia* did for sand.
JOHN SIMON

Parting Shots is essentially the equivalent of vanity publishing: a film directed by Michael Winner, produced by Michael Winner, written by Michael Winner, edited by Michael Winner, and made for Michael Winner to watch, perhaps in company with Michael Winner's current girlfriend.
MARK STEYN

The worst film of this or possibly any year.
BARRY TOOK, of *The Stickup*

Dustin Hoffman seems to have taken a correspondence course in playing gangsters from Al Pacino.
CHRISTOPHER TOOKEY, of *Billy Bathgate*

9½ Weeks put the rot back into erotica.
CHRISTOPHER TOOKEY

This film should never have been released, not even on parole.
CHRISTOPHER TOOKEY, of *Desperate Hours*

Forrest Gump is roughly as truthful about the world of intellectual handicap as *The Little Mermaid* is about fish.
CHRISTOPHER TOOKEY

The movie eventually seems to lose interest in the subject, though quite a bit later than the audience.
CHRISTOPHER TOOKEY, of 2006 culture clash movie *Prime*

Music

Anton Bruckner wrote the same symphony nine times, trying to get it right. He failed.
EDWARD ABBEY

I can't believe that girl bought her own engagement ring! I've seen it, up close. It looks like she got it on QVC. I know Britney. She's not trailer trash, but she sure acts that way.
CHRISTINA AGUILERA, of Britney Spears

Babyshambles have only ever released one song – one song! People talk about this great talent, but there's nothing to him. He's a mess.
DAMON ALBARN, of Pete Doherty

For *Everyone Says I Love You*, only Drew Barrymore's singing voice was dubbed. It was outside the limits of human tolerance.
WOODY ALLEN

Drew Barrymore sings so badly, deaf people refuse to watch her lips move.
WOODY ALLEN

Jack Benny played Mendelssohn last night. Mendelssohn lost.
ANON

Madonna sings like Mickey Mouse on helium.
ANON

One of those bands who make you want to stamp your feet – all over them.
ANON, of Westlife

I love Wagner, but the music I prefer is that of a cat hung up by its tail outside a window and trying to stick to the panes of glass with its claws.
CHARLES BAUDELAIRE

All Bach's last movements are like the running of a sewing machine.
ARNOLD BAX

The bagpipes sound exactly the same when you have finished learning them as when you start.
THOMAS BEECHAM

Brass bands are all very well in their place – outdoors and several miles away.
THOMAS BEECHAM

Music

No operatic tenor has yet died soon enough for me.
THOMAS BEECHAM

Beethoven's last quartets were written by a deaf man and should only be listened to by a deaf man.
THOMAS BEECHAM

It's like a lot of yaks jumping about.
THOMAS BEECHAM, of Beethoven's Seventh Symphony

The musical equivalent of St Pancras station.
THOMAS BEECHAM, of Edward Elgar

A glorified bandmaster.
THOMAS BEECHAM, of Arturo Toscanini

I liked your opera. I think I will set it to music.
LUDWIG VAN BEETHOVEN, to a fellow composer

Handel is a tub of pork and beer.
HECTOR BERLIOZ

Did I tell you about my nightmare? I dreamt I was Madonna, shopping at Tiffany's, where I was trying to buy some class.
SANDRA BERNHARD

I look at my friendship with Madonna as like having a gallstone. You deal with it, there is pain, and then you pass it.
SANDRA BERNHARD

Vanilla Ice was the Pat Boone of rap.
JELLO BIAFRA

From gaudy to grim to downright frenetic, these two prove
that bad taste is positively genetic.
MR BLACKWELL, of sisters Ashlee and Jessica Simpson

Britney Spears looks like an over-the-hill Lolita.
MR BLACKWELL

He was happily married – but his wife wasn't.
VICTOR BORGE, of Wolfgang Amadeus Mozart

It is gaudy musical harlotry, savage and incoherent bellow-
ings.
BOSTON GAZETTE, of Franz Liszt

Elton John is like our headmaster, the grand old dame of
pop, with a beautiful voice but living in an ornate bubble,
full of fresh flowers, surrounded by people who nod and
laugh at everything he says.
BOY GEORGE

If Madonna were a drag queen, she would be called Ruth
Less.
BOY GEORGE

Debussy played the piano with the lid down.
ROBERT BRESSON

He's got a chin like an ironing board.
PETE BURNS, of Lionel Richie

Mick Jagger moves like a parody between a majorette girl and Fred Astaire.
TRUMAN CAPOTE

I'd rather be onstage with a pig.
MARIAH CAREY, of Jennifer Lopez

It's hard work reviewing a Stereophonics album. For a start, it involves having to sit all the way through a Stereophonics album.
PETE CASHMORE

Berlioz composes by splashing his pen over the manuscript and leaving the issue to chance.
FREDERIC CHOPIN

Alban Berg's music is a soporific, by the side of which the telephone book is a strong cup of coffee.
SAMUEL CHOTZINOFF

If a horse could sing in a monotone, the horse would sound like Carly Simon, only a horse wouldn't rhyme "yacht", "apricot", and "gavotte".
ROBERT CHRISTGAU

Pete Doherty creates all this misery for himself to write songs and then doesn't even turn up to play them. And they're not that good anyway.
CHARLOTTE CHURCH

I can't stand Bob Dylan. He sounds like a freak.
CHARLOTTE CHURCH

That guy's voice just drones on and on – it's like bagpipes.
CHARLOTTE CHURCH, of Snow Patrol

Lonnie Donegan died in 2002 and Mark Knopfler and Rolf Harris played at his tribute show. Friends say it's what he would have wanted – to be dead at the time.
JULIAN CLARY

He has a woman's name and wears make-up. How original!
ALICE COOPER, of Marilyn Manson

Listening to the Fifth Symphony of Ralph Vaughan Williams is like staring at a cow for forty-five minutes.
AARON COPELAND

If reaching a larger market means that you have to sound like Christopher Cross, then I'd rather stay where I am.
ELVIS COSTELLO

There's no humour in his music and there doesn't seem to be much depth. It's the sort of thing you'd write on a card if you were sending flowers.
GRAHAM COXON, of James Blunt

I have seen Madonna up close. Neither the music nor the image inspires my loins.
DAVID COVERDALE

She can't sing, write or play an instrument to save her life.
DAVID CROSBY, of Britney Spears

All legs and hair with a mouth that could swallow the whole stadium and the hot-dog stand.
LAURA LEE DAVIES, of Tina Turner

How Garth Brooks achieved superstar status remains as much a mystery as the *Mary Celeste*.
FRED DELLAR

Berlioz, musically speaking, is a lunatic; a classical composer only in Paris, the great city of quacks.
DRAMATIC AND MUSICAL REVIEW

Composition indeed! Decomposition is the proper word for such hateful fungi.
DRAMATIC AND MUSICAL REVIEW, of Franz Liszt

Far too noisy, my dear Mozart, far too many notes.
ARCHDUKE FERDINAND OF AUSTRIA

He was ignored till he began to smash the parlour furniture, throw bombs and hitch together ten pianolas, all playing different tunes, whereupon everyone began to talk about him.
HENRY T. FINK, of Arnold Schönberg

Ozzy Osbourne couldn't carry a tune around in a suitcase.
RONNIE JAMES DIO

Robbie Williams? You mean that fat dancer from Take That?
NOEL GALLAGHER

Art Garfunkel makes Paul Simon look like LL Cool J.
IAN GITTINS

I think he sounds like some weird guy with fuzzy hair from
the Seventies.
ALISON GOLDFRAPP, of James Blunt

I met Bananarama once. They are living proof that make-
up works.
CHESNEY HAWKES

Their lyrics are unrecognisable as the Queen's English.
EDWARD HEATH, of the Beatles

Irving Berlin had a voice that sounded like a hoarse tomcat
with its tail in a clothes wringer.
BOB HOPE

Perry [Como] gave his usual impersonation of a man who
has been simultaneously told to say "cheese" and shot in
the back with a poisoned arrow.
CLIVE JAMES

Rod Stewart has an attractive voice and a highly unattractive bottom. He now spends more time wagging the latter
than exercising the former.
CLIVE JAMES

For the lifespan he's lasted, Chuck Berry's productivity has
been nil, more or less.
ELTON JOHN

Anyone who lip-synchs on stage when you pay £75 to see them should be shot.
ELTON JOHN, of Madonna

He's pathetic. It's like a monkey with arthritis trying to go on stage and look young. I have great respect for the Stones but they would have been better if they'd thrown Keith [Richards] out fifteen years ago.
ELTON JOHN

Feargal Sharkey has a face like a bucket with a dent in it.
ALLAN JONES

They've found a new chamber in the Great Pyramid. And here's what was on the wall: Rolling Stones Tour, 1567 BC.
CRAIG KILBORN

[Max] Reger's name is the same backwards or forwards, and his music displays the same characteristic.
IRVING KOLODIN

Luciano Pavarotti is only slightly smaller than Vermont.
NORMAN LEBRECHT

The Rolling Stones say their current US tour is a lot harder than their first, when we had only thirteen states.
JAY LENO

Play us a medley of your hit.
OSCAR LEVANT, to George Gershwin

The musical equivalent of blancmange.
BERNARD LEVIN, of Frederick Delius

She's like somebody's mum who'd a few too many drinks at a cocktail party.
NICK LOWE, of Grace Slick

Billy Idol: the Perry Como of Punk.
JOHN LYDON

That silly little goatee beard made him look like Acker Bilk's lovechild.
NIGEL LYTHGOE, of Darius

Christmas has gone, but the goose is still fat.
NIGEL LYTHGOE, of Kym Marsh

I don't think she's the brightest of buttons.
PAUL MCCARTNEY, of Yoko Ono

I am unable to see in [Bob] Dylan anything other than a youth of mediocre talent. Only a completely non-critical audience, nourished on the watery pap of pop music, could have fallen for such tenth-rate drivel.
EWAN MACCOLL

Kate Bush: sort of like the consequences of mating Patti Smith with a Hoover vacuum cleaner.
DAVE MCGEE

She looks like she's had a run-in with a lawnmower. She's about as sexy as a Venetian blind.
MADONNA, of Sinead O'Connor

Music

Elvis Costello looks like Buddy Holly after drinking a can of STP Oil Treatment.
DAVE MARSH

Fee Waybill of the Tubes had the most unique range in rock: two notes, both flat.
DAVE MARSH

Bananarama display the discreet choreography of a herd of clubfooted elephants.
MELODY MAKER

Michael Jackson hasn't just lost the plot, he's lost the whole library!
MELODY MAKER

Simply Red are just music for chartered accountants to court to in wine bars.
MELODY MAKER

Elvis [Presley] transcends his talent to the point of dispensing with it altogether.
GREIL MARCUS

He makes millions playing those old classics day in and day out, whereas my drive and passion is still about the future.
GEORGE MICHAEL, of Elton John

I hope Harry Secombe dies before me because I don't want him singing at my funeral.
SPIKE MILLIGAN

If I go round to someone's house and there's an Eric Clapton record [there], I just walk out.
JON MOSS

Is Wagner a human being at all? Is he not rather a disease?
FRIEDRICH NIETZSCHE

Yoko Ono's voice sounded like an eagle being goosed.
RALPH NOVAK

Michael Bolton says he now wants to become an opera singer, which is great, because now my dad and I can hate the same kind of music.
CONAN O'BRIEN

Celine Dion is moving to Belgium to prepare for her comeback tour. Belgium has announced it's moving to France.
CONAN O'BRIEN

Years of cosmetic surgery have transformed Michael Jackson into a pubescent Elizabeth Taylor.
ALLISON PEARSON

Bach on the wrong notes.
SERGEY PROKOFIEV, of Igor Stravinsky

Leonard Cohen's music gives you the feeling that your dog just died.
Q MAGAZINE

Few people know that the CIA is planning to cripple Iran by playing this album on special loudspeakers secretly parachuted into the country.
RECORD MIRROR, of the Bee Gees' 1988 album *ESP*

Frank Zappa couldn't write a decent song if you gave him a million and a year on an island in Greece.
LOU REED

I couldn't warm to him even if I was cremated next to him.
KEITH RICHARDS, of Chuck Berry

Elton John's writing is limited to songs for dead blondes.
KEITH RICHARDS

Olivia Newton-John is Australia's gift to insomniacs. It's nothing but the blonde singing the bland.
MINNIE RIPERTON

With Mick Jagger's lips, he could French-kiss a moose.
JOAN RIVERS

Madonna has just lost thirty pounds – she shaved her legs.
JOAN RIVERS

A nutcase in a bikini who last ate a carbohydrate in 1999.
JOHN ROBINSON, of Geri Halliwell

Eminem is the voice of a generation while Robbie Williams is just the voice of Robbie Williams.
PETER ROBINSON

If I had a hammer, I'd use it on Peter, Paul and Mary.
HOWARD ROSENBERG

In her shell suit she used to look like a single mum on a council estate.
JONATHAN ROSS, of Spice Girl Mel C

Wagner had some wonderful moments but awful quarter-hours.
GIOACCHINO ROSSINI

Beethoven always sounds like the upsetting of bags – with here and there a dropped hammer.
JOHN RUSKIN

Madonna is like a McDonald's hamburger. When you ask for a Big Mac, you know exactly what you're getting. It's enjoyable, but it satisfies only for the moment.
SADE

If Cher has another facelift she'll be wearing a beard.
JENNIFER SAUNDERS

The audience seemed rather disappointed: they expected the ocean, something big, something colossal, but they were served instead with some agitated water in a saucer.
LOUIS SCHNEIDER, of Claude Debussy's *La Mer*

When [Maria] Callas carried a grudge, she planted it, nursed it, fostered it, watered it, and watched it grow to sequoia size.
HAROLD C. SCHONBERG

Most of all he gives me the impression of being a spoilt child.
CLARA SCHUMANN, of Franz Liszt

He still persists in making records that have all the unhinged beatnik wildness of a Neighbourhood Watch meeting.
VICTORIA SEGAL, of Paul McCartney's desire to be seen as bohemian

His wantonness is not vicious. It is that of a great baby, rather tirelessly addicted to dressing himself up as Handel or Beethoven and making a prolonged and intolerable noise.
GEORGE BERNARD SHAW, of Johannes Brahms

There are some experiences in life which should not be demanded twice from any man, and one of them is listening to the Brahms *Requiem*.
GEORGE BERNARD SHAW

Kiri te Kanawa: a viable alternative to valium.
IRA SIFF

His kind of music is deplorable, a rancid-smelling aphrodisiac.
FRANK SINATRA, of Elvis Presley

A man with the face of an Internet dweeb and the dress sense of a teacher.
MIMI SPENCER, of Chris Martin

Harpists spend ninety per cent of their lives tuning their harps and ten per cent playing out of tune.
IGOR STRAVINSKY

Vivaldi is greatly overrated – a dull fellow who could compose the same form over and so many times over.
IGOR STRAVINSKY

I can compare *Le Carnival Romain* by Berlioz to nothing but the caperings and gibberings of a big baboon, over-excited by a dose of alcoholic stimulus.
GEORGE TEMPLETON STRONG

Michael Jackson now looks like a Barbie doll that has been whittled at by a malicious brother.
THOMAS SUTCLIFFE

Tom Jones has earned a permanent niche in the annals of nursing-home rock.
JOHN SWENSON

Frederick Delius: a provincial Debussy.
A.J.P. TAYLOR

Brahms has no charm for me. I find him cold and obscure, full of pretensions, but without any real depth.
PYOTR TCHAIKOVSKY

Handel is only fourth-rate. He is not even interesting.
PYOTR TCHAIKOVSKY

Wagner's music is better than it sounds.
MARK TWAIN

Frankie Laine's approach to the microphone is that of an accused man pleading with a hostile jury.
KENNETH TYNAN

There are people who are fanatical about Celine Dion. These are the same folks who mourn the demise of Watney's Red Barrel and *The Black and White Minstrel Show* and were a tad upset that Michael Bolton shaved the mullet.
STEVEN WELLS

I like Wagner's music better than anybody's. It is so loud that one can talk the whole time without people hearing what one says.
OSCAR WILDE

To Noel Gallagher, RIP. Heard your latest album – with deepest sympathy.
ROBBIE WILLIAMS

It must be great being Bryan Adams. You just carry on living in your world of three chords, a chorus and simple "Feels so right, can't be wrong" sentiments.
JIM WIRTH

There is absolutely nothing wrong with Oscar Levant that a miracle cannot fix.
ALEXANDER WOOLLCOTT

[Mick] Jagger's sold out. His music is boring and he didn't deserve his knighthood. And he still can't forgive the fact I've had more lovers than him.
BILL WYMAN

Boy George reminds me of an aubergine – all shiny and plump.
PAUL YOUNG

Politics

[Richard] Nixon impeached himself. He gave us Gerald Ford as his revenge.
BELLA ABZUG

[Charles] Sumner's mind had reached the calm of water which receives and reflects images without absorbing them; it contained nothing but itself.
HENRY ADAMS

Jimmy [Carter]'s basic problem is that he's super cautious. He looks before and after he leaps.
JOEY ADAMS

A barbarian who cannot write a sentence of grammar and can hardly spell his own name.
JOHN QUINCY ADAMS, of Andrew Jackson

His principles are all subordinate to his ambitions.
JOHN QUINCY ADAMS, of Martin Van Buren

Frankly, if I was going to recruit somebody, I'd go further up the gene pool.
REG ALCOCK, of Canadian politician Inky Mark

That George Washington was not a scholar is certain. That he is too illiterate, unlearned, unread for his station is equally beyond dispute.
JOHN ADAMS

He can't even speak. I just find him an embarrassment.
ROBERT ALTMAN, of George W. Bush

For twenty years he has held a season ticket on the line of least resistance, and has gone wherever the train of events has carried him, lucidly justifying his position at whatever point he has happened to find himself.
LEO AMERY, of Herbert Asquith

First in ability on the list of second-rate men.
ANON, of Chester Arthur

There are two sides to every question and he always takes both.
ANON, of Paddy Ashdown

I don't think Kenneth Baker has his hair cut; he just has an oil change.
ANON

Aneurin Bevan can hardly enter a railway train because there is no Fourth Class.
ANON

Cherie Blair has a mouth best suited to sitting on a lily pad.
ANON

You can tell when Tony Blair is lying – his lips are moving.
ANON

Rhodes Boyson looks like a character out of an unpublished novel by Charles Dickens.
ANON

When Gordon Brown leaves a room, the lights go on.
ANON

Bill Clinton is the Karaoke Kid – he'd sing anything to get elected.
ANON

He is so silent that he is always worth listening to.
ANON, of Calvin Coolidge

She has all the charm and finesse of a sledgehammer.
ANON, of Gwyneth Dunwoody

He won't leave any footprints on the sands of time because he is too busy covering his tracks.
ANON, of Roy Hattersley

[Herbert] Hoover isn't a stuffed shirt. But at times he can give the most convincing impersonation of a stuffed shirt you ever saw.
ANON

Gerald Kaufman started by trying to move mountains, but ended up by merely throwing dirt.
ANON

Neil Kinnock thinks bullshit baffles brains.
ANON

He could not tell the difference between pulling one's leg and breaking it.
ANON, of Selwyn Lloyd

John Major delivers all his statements as though auditioning for the speaking clock.
ANON

The United States has Ronald Reagan, Johnny Cash, Bob Hope and Stevie Wonder. New Zealand has Robert Muldoon, no cash, no hope, and no wonder!
ANON, of Robert Muldoon

Robert Muldoon is a bull who carries his own china shop with him.
ANON

John Prescott keeps behaving like an untipped waiter.
ANON

The only way John Prescott could make a girl go weak at the knees is by sitting on them.
ANON

Dan Quayle looks like Robert Redford's retarded brother that they kept in the attic, and he got out somehow.
ANON

Shirley Summerskill has a face like a well-kept grave.
ANON

Margaret Thatcher objects to ideas only when others have them.
ANON

Peace, prosperity and a president smarter than his dog – already the Clinton years seem a golden age by comparison
ARKANSAS TIMES

Say what you like about the President, but we know his friends have convictions.
DICK ARMEY, of Bill Clinton

The manners of a cad and the tongue of a bargee.
HERBERT ASQUITH, of Joseph Chamberlain

Sir Stafford Cripps has a brilliant mind until it is made up.
LADY ASQUITH

He can't see a belt without hitting below it.
MARGOT ASQUITH, of David Lloyd George

The trouble with Winston [Churchill] is that he nails his trousers to the mast and can't climb down.
CLEMENT ATTLEE

If he were a horse, nobody would buy him; with that eye no one could answer for his temper.
WALTER BAGEHOT, of Lord Brougham

He has conferred on the practice of vacillation the aura of statesmanship.
KENNETH BAKER, of David Owen

Lloyd George spent his whole life plastering together the true and the false and therefrom manufacturing the plausible.
STANLEY BALDWIN

He is undoubtedly proof that a pig's bladder on a stick can be elected as a Member of Parliament.
TONY BANKS, of Terry Dicks

Listening to Terry Dicks opining on the arts is rather like listening to Vlad the Impaler presenting *Blue Peter*.
TONY BANKS

At one moment [Michael] Portillo was polishing his jackboots and planning the advance. Next thing he shows up as a TV presenter. It is rather like Pol Pot joining the Teletubbies.
TONY BANKS

[Winston] Churchill on top of the wave has in him the stuff of which tyrants are made.
LORD BEAVERBROOK

Clement Attlee brings to the fierce struggle of politics the tepid enthusiasm of a lazy summer afternoon at a cricket match.
ANEURIN BEVAN

This second-rate orator trails his tawdry wisps of mist over the parliamentary scene.
ANEURIN BEVAN, of Stanley Baldwin

The worst thing I can say about democracy is that it has tolerated the right honourable gentleman for four and a half years.
ANEURIN BEVAN, of Neville Chamberlain

His ear is so sensitively attuned to the bugle note of history that he is often deaf to the more raucous clamour of modern life.
ANEURIN BEVAN, of Winston Churchill

The Prime Minister has an absolute genius for putting flamboyant labels on empty luggage.
ANEURIN BEVAN, of Harold Macmillan

I think [Stanley] Baldwin has gone mad. He simply takes one jump in the dark, looks around and then takes another.
LORD BIRKENHEAD

He rushes into a fight with the horns of a bull and the skin of a rabbit.
JEREMIAH BLACK, of James Garfield

A becurled and perfumed grandee gazed at by the gallery-gapers.
JAMES G. BLAINE, of Roscoe Conkling

We knew George W. Bush was in the oil business – we just didn't know it was snake oil.
JULIAN BOND

John Prescott looks like a terrifying mixture of Hannibal Lecter and Terry Scott.
GYLES BRANDRETH

[Benjamin] Disraeli is a self-made man who worships his creator.
JOHN BRIGHT

He is a man of his most recent word.
WILLIAM F. BUCKLEY JR, of Lyndon B. Johnson

[Richard] Nixon is a man who had the morals of a private detective.
WILLIAM S. BURROUGHS

He's the stealth candidate. His campaign jets from place to place, but no issues show up on the radar screen.
GEORGE BUSH SR, of Michael Dukakis

Michael Portillo is so wooden, he should be creosoted.
GARRY BUSHELL

It was very good of God to let Thomas and Mrs Carlyle marry one another and so make only two people miserable instead of four.
SAMUEL BUTLER

Ronald Reagan doesn't dye his hair, he bleaches his face.
JOHNNY CARSON

Ronald Reagan is slightly to the right of the Sheriff of Nottingham.
JOHNNY CARSON

He is a sheep in sheep's clothing.
WINSTON CHURCHILL, of Clement Attlee

A modest little man with much to be modest about.
WINSTON CHURCHILL, of Clement Attlee

He occasionally stumbles over the truth, but he always hastily picks himself up and hurries on as if nothing had happened.
WINSTON CHURCHILL, of Stanley Baldwin

Decided only to be undecided, resolved to be irresolute, adamant for drift, solid for fluidity, all-powerful to be impotent.
WINSTON CHURCHILL, of Stanley Baldwin

I've just learnt about his illness; let's hope it's nothing trivial.
WINSTON CHURCHILL, of Aneurin Bevan

He looked at foreign affairs through the wrong end of a municipal drainpipe.
WINSTON CHURCHILL, of Neville Chamberlain

He looked like a female llama surprised in her bath.
WINSTON CHURCHILL, of Charles de Gaulle

The greatest cross I have to bear is the cross of Lorraine.
WINSTON CHURCHILL, of Charles de Gaulle

He has, more than any other man, the gift of compressing the largest amount of words into the smallest amount of thought.
WINSTON CHURCHILL, of Ramsay MacDonald

Bill Clinton is a man who thinks international affairs means dating a girl from out of town.
TOM CLANCY

If life were fair, Dan Quayle would be making a living asking, "Do you want fries with that?"
JOHN CLEESE

Mr [Woodrow] Wilson bores me with his fourteen points; why, God Almighty has only ten.
GEORGES CLEMENCEAU

The rogue elephant of Australian politics.
E.H. COLLIS, of William Lyne

Calvin Coolidge's perpetual expression was that of someone smelling something burning on a stove.
SHERWIN L. COOK

That man has offered me unsolicited advice for six years, all of it bad.
CALVIN COOLIDGE, of Herbert Hoover

Richard Nixon's motto was: "If two wrongs don't make a right, try three."
NORMAN COUSINS

Michael Heseltine could not see a parapet without ducking beneath it.
JULIAN CRITCHLEY

Margaret Thatcher cannot see an institution without hitting it with her handbag.
JULIAN CRITCHLEY

It is better to be sincere in one language than to be a twit in two.
JOHN CROSBIE, of Pierre Trudeau

The only man, woman or child who wrote a simple declarative sentence with seven grammatical errors, is dead.
E.E. CUMMINGS, of Warren G. Harding

Small, short-sighted, blonde, barbed – she reminds me of a bright little hedgehog.
EDWINA CURRIE, of Teresa Gorman

He does not march, nor quite walk, but pitches along as if the next step would bring him on his nose.
RICHARD DANA, of Ulysses S. Grant

He is a man whose contribution to the arts is about the same as Bluebeard's contribution to the institution of marriage.
TERRY DICKS, of Tony Banks

Randolph Churchill is like a minute insect which bites without being felt.
BENJAMIN DISRAELI

He has not a single redeeming defect.
BENJAMIN DISRAELI, of William Ewart Gladstone

A misfortune is if Gladstone fell into the Thames; a calamity would be if someone pulled him out.
BENJAMIN DISRAELI

The right honourable gentleman is reminiscent of a poker. The only difference is that a poker gives off the occasional signs of warmth.
BENJAMIN DISRAELI, of Sir Robert Peel

The right honourable gentleman's smile is like the silver fittings on a coffin.
BENJAMIN DISRAELI, of Sir Robert Peel

If a traveller were informed that such a man was Leader of the House of Commons, he might begin to comprehend how the Egyptians worshipped an insect.
BENJAMIN DISRAELI, of Lord John Russell

When Edwina Currie goes to the dentist, he's the one who needs the anaesthetic.
FRANK DOBSON

No wonder that girl was licking David Mellor's toes. She was probably trying to get as far away from his face as possible.
TOMMY DOCHERTY

Tony Blair has done more U-turns than a dodgy plumber.
IAIN DUNCAN SMITH

Most presidents are figureheads; [George W.] Bush is a hood ornament.
WILL DURST

Walter Mondale has all the charisma of a speed bump.
WILL DURST

He struts sitting down.
LILLIAN K. DYKESTRA, of Thomas Dewey

Someday our grandchildren will look up at us and say, "Where were you, Grandma, and what were you doing when you first realised that President Reagan was, er, not playing with a full deck?"
BARBARA EHRENREICH

A senescent bimbo with a lust for home furnishings.
BARBARA EHRENREICH, of Nancy Reagan

President [George W.] Bush wrote a letter offering his condolences to the wife of a missing Chinese fighter pilot. After Bush wrote the letter, it was quickly given to experts and then translated. Then it was translated into Chinese.
JIMMY FALLON

It is not necessary that every time he rises he should give his famous imitation of a semi-house-trained polecat.
MICHAEL FOOT, of Norman Tebbit

Jimmy Carter wants to speak loudly and carry a fly swatter.
GERALD FORD

George W. Bush: this is a guy who could not find oil in Texas.
AL FRANKEN

Gerald Ford looks like the guy in a science-fiction movie who is the first to see the Creature.
DAVID FRYE

When he rises to speak, he does not know what he is going to say. When he is speaking he does not know what he is saying, and when he sits down he does not know what he has said.
WILLIAM EWART GLADSTONE, of Lord Derby

James G. Blaine wallowed in corruption like a rhinoceros in an African pool.
E.L. GODKIN

Dan Quayle is more stupid than Ronald Reagan put together.
MATT GROENING

It is said he is a disgusting man to do business with. Coarse, dirty, clownish in his address and stiff and abstracted in his opinions, which are drawn from books exclusively.
WILLIAM HENRY HARRISON, of John Quincy Adams

A posturing old bully.
MAX HASTINGS, of Donald Rumsfeld

George W. Bush has achieved the unusual feat of being simultaneously sinister and ridiculous.
ROY HATTERSLEY

Malcolm Fraser could be described as a cutlery man – he was born with a silver spoon in his mouth and he uses it to stab his colleagues in the back.
BOB HAWKE

He had a heavyweight intellect with a lightweight judgement.
DENIS HEALEY, of Richard Crossman

Being attacked in the House by him is like being savaged by a dead sheep.
DENIS HEALEY, of Geoffrey Howe

A mixture of Rasputin and Tommy Cooper.
DENIS HEALEY, of Sir Keith Joseph

Margaret Thatcher: a bargain-basement Boadicea.
DENIS HEALEY

The Prime Minister has given the French President a piece of her mind, not a gift I would receive with alacrity.
DENIS HEALEY, of Margaret Thatcher

We need a President who's fluent in at least one language.
BUCK HENRY, of George Bush

Paddy Ashdown transformed a party without a leader into a party without a leader.
MICHAEL HESELTINE.

A lager lout.
MICHAEL HESELTINE, of John Prescott

The self-appointed king of the gutter.
MICHAEL HESELTINE, of Neil Kinnock

If ignorance goes to forty dollars a barrel, I want drilling rights to George Bush's head.
JIM HIGHTOWER

Harry S. Truman rules the country with an iron fist, the same way he plays the piano.
BOB HOPE

He would rather follow public opinion than lead it.
HARRY HOPKINS, of Franklin D. Roosevelt

One could drive a schooner through any part of his argument and never scrape against a fact.
DAVID HOUSTON, of William Jennings Bryan

He suggests, preposterously, that I sneer at ministers – he knows a great deal about that because he's done it for a long time.
JOHN HUMPHRYS, of Alastair Campbell

He is distrustful, obstinate, excessively vain, and takes no counsel from anyone.
THOMAS JEFFERSON, of John Adams

Gerry Ford is a nice guy but he played too much football with his helmet off.
LYNDON B. JOHNSON

The enviably attractive nephew who sings an Irish ballad for the company and then winsomely disappears before the table-clearing and dishwashing begin.
LYNDON B. JOHNSON, of John F. Kennedy

Al Gore has less star quality than head lice.
JOE JOSEPH

Like a lizard on a rock – alive, but looking dead.
PAUL KEATING, of John Hewson

He's like a stone statue in the cemetery.
PAUL KEATING, of John Hewson

Like being flogged with a warm lettuce.
PAUL KEATING, on being verbally attacked by John Hewson

John Howard has more hide than a team of elephants.
PAUL KEATING

What we have here is an intellectual rust bucket.
PAUL KEATING, of Andrew Peacock

It's funny to watch this clueless man go through the motions.
GARRISON KEILLOR, of George W. Bush

Ronald Reagan must love poor people because he's creating so many more of them.
EDWARD KENNEDY

Do you realise the responsibility I carry? I'm the only person between [Richard] Nixon and the White House.
JOHN F. KENNEDY, 1960

He is a ditherer and a dodger, a ducker and weaver.
NEIL KINNOCK, of John Major

George W. Bush is clearly the best thing to happen to political humorists since . . .well, since Bill Clinton.
DANIEL KURTZMAN

He's probably been delayed by a full-length mirror.
DAVID LANGE, of Winston Peters

He looked at me as if I was a side dish he hadn't ordered.
RING LARDNER, of William Taft

In Pierre Elliott Trudeau, Canada has at last produced a political leader worthy of assassination.
IRVING LAYTON

When [Henry] Kissinger can get the Nobel Peace Prize, what is there left for satire?
TOM LEHRER

[George W.] Bush said today he is being stalked. He said wherever he goes, people are following him. Finally someone told him, "Psst, that's the Secret Service."
JAY LENO

What a nightmare I had last night. I dreamed I was at a Washington party and I had to choose between Dick Cheney taking me on a hunting trip or Ted Kennedy driving me home.
JAY LENO

President [George W.] Bush says he needs a month off to unwind. Unwind? When the hell does this guy wind?
DAVID LETTERMAN

For those of you who wondered what a Dan Quayle presidency would have been like, now you know!
DAVID LETTERMAN, of George W. Bush

Arnold Schwarzenegger is the first body builder to run for governor since Janet Reno.
DAVID LETTERMAN

Des Browne is not a man to walk past a mirror without casting it an admiring glance.
QUENTIN LETTS

Gwyneth Dunwoody: a heavy roller who flattens all ministerial earthworms.
QUENTIN LETTS

A night-club bouncer with narrow eyes, a fist fighter's twitch and a pre-emptive hint of rage.
QUENTIN LETTS, of John Reid

He is about as saleable as a carton of sour milk.
QUENTIN LETTS, of John Reid

Once he makes up his mind, he's full of indecision.
OSCAR LEVANT, of Dwight D. Eisenhower

It was almost impossible to believe he was anything but a down-at-heel actor resting between engagements at the decrepit theatres of minor provincial towns.
BERNARD LEVIN, of Harold Macmillan

There, but for the grace of Pierre Elliott Trudeau, sits God.
DAVID LEWIS

He is a man totally unfitted for the position. His principles are elastic, and he is careless with the truth.
JOHN L. LEWIS, of Harry S. Truman

I wouldn't waste the twenty-five cents to buy the cartridge that would propel the bullet.
G. GORDON LIDDY, of John Dean

His argument is as thin as the homeopathic soup that was made by boiling the shadow of a pigeon that had been starved to death.
ABRAHAM LINCOLN, of Stephen A. Douglas

He's the kind of guy you'd like to have around when you want to be alone. With a little effort he could become an anonymity.
RICH LITTLE, of George Bush

Margaret Beckett looks like a woman resigned to walk home alone to an empty bedsit after Grab-a-Granny night at the local disco.
RICHARD LITTLEJOHN

He reacts to even the most innocuous question with an invitation to step outside.
RICHARD LITTLEJOHN, of John Prescott

John Prescott has a wholly justified inferiority complex. He's got plenty to feel inferior about.
RICHARD LITTLEJOHN

He might make an adequate Lord Mayor of Birmingham in a lean year.
DAVID LLOYD GEORGE, of Neville Chamberlain

A retail mind in a wholesale business.
DAVID LLOYD GEORGE, of Neville Chamberlain

He has half a dozen solutions to any problem and one of them is right – the trouble is he does not know which it is.
DAVID LLOYD GEORGE, of Winston Churchill

Sufficient conscience to bother him, but not sufficient to keep him straight.
DAVID LLOYD GEORGE, of Ramsay MacDonald

The right honourable and learned gentleman has twice crossed the floor of this House, each time leaving behind a trail of slime.
DAVID LLOYD GEORGE, of Sir John Simon

He looks like a Kinder egg with no toy inside.
SEAN LOCK, of Iain Duncan Smith

I do wish he didn't look as if he had been weaned on a pickle.
ALICE ROOSEVELT LONGWORTH, of Calvin Coolidge

No woman has ever so comforted the distressed – or so distressed the comfortable.
CLARE BOOTHE LUCE, of Eleanor Roosevelt

His speeches leave the impression of an army of pompous phrases moving over the landscape in search of an idea.
WILLIAM MCADOO, of Warren G. Harding

Richard Nixon is the kind of guy who, if you were drowning twenty feet from shore, would throw you a fifteen-foot rope.
EUGENE MCCARTHY

Richard Nixon was like a kamikaze pilot who keeps apologising for the attack.
MARY MCGRORY

He suffers from what you may regard as a fatal defect in a Chancellor. He is always wrong.
IAIN MACLEOD, of James Callaghan

Double-talk is his mother tongue. He is a man whose vision is limited to tomorrow's headlines.
IAIN MACLEOD, of Harold Wilson

Anthony Eden is forever poised between a cliché and an indiscretion.
HAROLD MACMILLAN

He behaves like an agitated parrot with constipation.
JOHN MAJOR, of Frank Dobson

The chameleon of politics, consistent only in his inconsistency.
JOHN MAJOR, of Neil Kinnock

I believe that Ronald Reagan can make this country what it once was – an Arctic region covered with ice.
STEVE MARTIN

She's upstairs filing her teeth.
GROUCHO MARX, of Eleanor Roosevelt

John Major makes George Bush seem like a personality.
JACKIE MASON

When I arrived at the Environment Ministry in 1997, John Prescott thought biodiversity was a kind of washing powder.
MICHAEL MEACHER

Grover Cleveland sailed through American history like a steel ship loaded with monoliths of granite.
H.L. MENCKEN

A tin-horn politician with the manner of a rural corn doctor and the mien of a ham actor.
H.L. MENCKEN, of Warren G. Harding

He had every quality that morons esteem in their heroes.
H.L. MENCKEN, of Franklin D. Roosevelt

He hated all pretensions, save his own pretensions.
H. L. MENCKEN, of Theodore Roosevelt

Nancy Reagan has agreed to be the world's first artificial heart donor.
ANDREA MICHAELS

She's democratic enough to talk down to anyone.
AUSTIN MITCHELL, of Margaret Thatcher

Lyndon Johnson turned out to be so many different characters he could have populated all of *War and Peace* and still had a few people left over.
HERBERT MITGANG

Margaret Thatcher has the mouth of Marilyn Monroe and the eyes of Caligula.
FRANÇOIS MITTERAND

Tony Blair does the work of two men – Laurel and Hardy.
BOB MONKHOUSE

He's not the most charismatic personality. In school his nickname was "Iain".
BOB MONKHOUSE, of Iain Duncan Smith

She's not my cup of tea. If I ever see her again, it will be too soon.
PIERS MORGAN, of Cherie Blair

Hyperbole was to Lyndon Johnson what oxygen is to life.
BILL MOYERS

The battle for the mind of Ronald Reagan was like the trench warfare of World War One: never have so many fought so hard for such barren terrain.
PEGGY NOONAN

President George W. Bush was in South Dakota today. There was an awkward moment at Mount Rushmore when he said: "Hey, look, it's those guys on the money!"
CONAN O'BRIEN

If I saw Mr [Charles] Haughey buried at midnight at a crossroads with a stake driven through his heart – politically speaking – I should continue to wear a clove of garlic around my neck, just in case.
CONAN O'BRIEN

Tabloids are reporting that Senator Ted Kennedy has an illegitimate twenty-one-year-old son. Apparently, Kennedy isn't denying the report, but the kid is.
CONAN O'BRIEN

One could not even dignify him with the name of a stuffed shirt. He was simply a hole in the air.
GEORGE ORWELL, of Stanley Baldwin

He reminds me of nothing so much as a dead fish before it has had time to stiffen.
GEORGE ORWELL, of Clement Attlee

The air currents of the world never ventilated his mind.
WALTER H. PAGE, of Woodrow Wilson

As he rose like a rocket, so he fell like a stick.
THOMAS PAINE, of Edmund Burke

How can they tell?
DOROTHY PARKER, on learning that Calvin Coolidge had died

Margaret Beckett is about as charming as Dracula's maiden auntie.
ALLISON PEARSON

Labour is trying to blame the Conservatives for John Prescott's affair. They say it's all Margaret Thatcher's fault for banning free eye tests.
ALLISON PEARSON

An empty suit that goes to funerals and plays golf.
ROSS PEROT, of Dan Quayle

All that glitters isn't [Philip] Gould.
JOHN PRESCOTT

Never was ability so much below mediocrity so well rewarded; no, not even when Caligula's horse was made a consul.
JOHN RANDOLPH, of Richard Rush

Richard Nixon inherited some good instincts from his Quaker forebears, but by diligent hard work, he overcame them.
JAMES RESTON

Dangerous as an enemy, untrustworthy as a friend, but fatal as a colleague.
SIR HERCULES ROBINSON, of Joseph Chamberlain

Calvin Coolidge didn't say much, and when he did he didn't say much.
WILL ROGERS

William McKinley has no more backbone than a chocolate éclair.
THEODORE ROOSEVELT

He has been called a mediocre man, but this is unwarranted flattery.
THEODORE ROOSEVELT, of John Tyler

The indefatigable air of a village apothecary inspecting the tongue of the State.
LORD ROSEBERY, of Henry Addington

When Bob Dole does smile, he looks as if he's just evicted a widow.
MIKE ROYKO

No man in our annals has filled so large a space and left it so empty.
CHARLES E. RUSSELL, of James G. Blaine

It is said that the President is willing to laugh at himself. That is fine, but when is he going to extend that privilege to us?
MORT SAHL, of John F. Kennedy

Would you buy a second-hand car from this man?
MORT SAHL, of Richard Nixon

We've got the kind of president who thinks arms control means some kind of deodorant.
PATRICIA SCHROEDER, of Ronald Reagan

Tony Blair is the ultimate air guitarist of modern political rhetoric.
WILL SELF

His idea of getting hold of the right end of the stick is to snatch it from the hands of somebody who is using it effectively, and to hit him over the head with it.
GEORGE BERNARD SHAW, of Theodore Roosevelt

The right honourable gentleman is indebted to his memory for his jests and to his imagination for his facts.
RICHARD BRINSLEY SHERIDAN, of Henry Dundas

Thomas Jefferson founded the Democratic Party; Franklin Roosevelt dumbfounded it.
DEWEY SHORT

Jimmy Carter had the air of a man who had never taken any decisions in his life. They had always been taken for him.
GUY SIMON

Winston [Churchill] has devoted the best years of his life to preparing his impromptu speeches.
F.E. SMITH

Gerald Ford looks and talks like he just fell off Edgar Bergen's lap.
DAVID STEINBERG

If I talk over people's heads, Ike must talk under their feet.
ADLAI STEVENSON, of Dwight D. Eisenhower

Richard Nixon is the kind of politician who would cut down a redwood tree, then mount its stump for a speech on conservation.
ADLAI STEVENSON

When one has peeled off the brown-paper wrapping of phrases and compromises, just nothing at all.
LYTTON STRACHEY, of Herbert Asquith

I feel certain that Woodrow Wilson would not recognise a generous impulse if he met it in the street.
WILLIAM TAFT

I regard him as a ruthless hypocrite and as an opportunist, who has no convictions he would not barter at once for votes.
WILLIAM TAFT, of Woodrow Wilson

He appears to have no clear political view except that the world should be a nicer place and that he should be loved and trusted by everyone and questioned by no one.
NORMAN TEBBIT, of Tony Blair

He does have the air of a chicken pecking at a lot of corn on the ground when he is speaking.
NORMAN TEBBIT, of Neil Kinnock

A brain-damaged old vulture.
HUNTER S. THOMPSON, of Hubert Humphrey

This fellow doesn't know any more about politics than a pig knows about Sunday.
HARRY S. TRUMAN, of Dwight D. Eisenhower

At a time when we needed a strong man, what we got was a man who swayed with the slightest breeze.
HARRY S. TRUMAN, of Millard Fillmore

He's one of the few in the history of the country to run for high office talking out of both sides of his mouth at the same time – and lying out of both sides.
HARRY S. TRUMAN, of Richard Nixon

I know for a fact that Mr Reagan is not clear about the difference between the Medici and the Gucci. He knows that Nancy wears one.
GORE VIDAL

I cannot bring myself to vote for a woman who has been voice-trained to speak to me as though my dog has just died.
KEITH WATERHOUSE, of Margaret Thatcher

I am suspicious of a man who has a handshake like a ten-cent pickled mackerel in brown paper.
WILLIAM A. WHITE, of Woodrow Wilson

He has something of the night about him.
ANN WIDDECOMBE, of Michael Howard

Harold Wilson is going round the country stirring up apathy.
WILLIAM WHITELAW

Bill Clinton is most comfortable when thinking about little things – school uniforms, the minimum wage and, above all, himself.
GEORGE F. WILL

Satire is alive and well and living in the White House.
ROBIN WILLIAMS

A shiver looking for a spine to run up.
HAROLD WILSON, of Edward Heath

A nonentity with sidewhiskers.
WOODROW WILSON, of Chester Arthur

He combined great gifts with great mediocrity.
WOODROW WILSON, of Ulysses S. Grant

Royalty

Ambition radiates off [Paul] Burrell like molten lava.
ANON

In private life he would be called an honest blockhead.
ANON, of George I

Throughout the greater part of his life, George III was a kind of consecrated obstruction.
WALTER BAGEHOT

A bossy, unattractive, galumphing girl.
CECIL BEATON, of Princess Anne

The Duke of Edinburgh has perfected the art of saying hello and goodbye in the same handshake.
JENNIE BOND

The Duke of Windsor was an extremely dull man. He even danced a boring Charleston, which is no mean feat.
NOËL COWARD

Royalty

The plain truth is that he was a most intolerable ruffian, a disgrace to human nature, and a blot of blood and grease upon the history of England.
CHARLES DICKENS, of Henry VIII

Short on looks, absolutely deprived of any dress sense, has a figure like a Jurassic monster.
NICHOLAS FAIRBURN, of Sarah Ferguson, Duchess of York

Born into the ranks of the working class, the new king's most likely fate would have been that of a street-corner loafer.
JAMES KEIR HARDIE, of George V

You have sent me a Flanders mare.
HENRY VIII, of Anne of Cleves

Henry IV's feet and armpits enjoyed an international reputation.
ALDOUS HUXLEY

I'm prepared to take advice on leisure from Prince Philip. He's a world expert on leisure. He's been practising for most of his adult life.
NEIL KINNOCK

The Billy Carter of the British monarchy.
ROBERT LACEY, of Princess Margaret

Not a bookish fellow and perhaps drinks more than is good for him.
QUENTIN LETTS, of Prince Harry

A dull, stupid and profligate king, full of drink and low conversation.
JUSTIN MCCARTHY, of George I

A very pleasant middle- to upper-class-type lady with a talkative retired Navy husband.
MALCOLM MUGGERIDGE, of Queen Elizabeth II

I found it ironic to hear the Queen reading her speech about abolishing fox hunting to Parliament with a dead stoat wrapped around her neck. But that's not a nice way to talk about the Duke of Edinburgh.
PAUL MERTON

Princess Margaret looked like a huge ball of fur on two well-developed legs.
NANCY MITFORD

For seventeen years he did nothing at all but kill animals and stick in stamps.
HAROLD NICOLSON, of George V

Prince Charles does a terrific job . . . for the Republican movement.
JOHN O'FARRELL

A noble, nasty course he ran,
Superbly filthy and fastidious;
He was the world's "first gentleman",
And made the appellation hideous.
WINTHROP MACKWORTH PRAED, of George IV

Royalty

Nowadays a parlour maid as ignorant as Queen Victoria was when she came to the throne would be classed as mentally defective.
GEORGE BERNARD SHAW

She's not a real princess, she's a slap-them-on-the-bottom princess.
EARL SPENCER, of Sarah Ferguson, Duchess of York

Sport

Baseball

He was frank to the point of cruelty and subtle as a belch.
LEE ALLEN, of Rogers Hornsby

A chunky, unshaven hobo who ran the bases like a berserk locomotive, slept in the raw, and swore at pitchers in his sleep.
LEE ALLEN, of Pepper Martin

He is quick on the bases, but this is an attribute that is about as essential for catchers as neat handwriting.
ROGER ANGELL, of Choo Choo Coleman

José Canseco is an attention-grabbing crackpot with the credibility of a street-corner snitch.
BRYAN BURWELL

Could be that Bill Terry's a nice guy when you get to know him, but why bother?
DIZZY DEAN

He's even-tempered. He comes to the ballpark mad and stays that way.
JOE GARAGIOLA, of Rick Burleson

He'd give you the shirt off his back. Of course, he'd call a press conference to announce it.
CATFISH HUNTER, of Reggie Jackson

[Stan] Musial's batting stance looks like a small boy looking around a corner to see if the cops are coming.
TED LYONS

When [Tom] Seaver laughs, he makes dogs whine.
LINDSEY NELSON

How can anyone as slow as you pull a muscle?
PETE ROSE, to Tony Perez

Pete Rose is the most likeable arrogant person I've ever met.
MIKE SCHMIDT

Boxing

I've seen George Foreman shadow boxing, and the shadow won.
MUHAMMAD ALI

He's so ugly they ought to donate his face to the World Wildlife Fund.
MUHAMMAD ALI, of Joe Frazier

He's so ugly that when he cries the tears run down the back of his head.
MUHAMMAD ALI, of Sonny Liston

When promoter Bob Arum pats you on the back, he's just looking for a spot to stick the knife.
CUS D'AMATO

He was nicknamed "Rembrandt" because he spent so much time on the canvas.
ANON

Some people say George [Foreman] is fit as a fiddle, but I think he looks more like a cello.
LOU DUVA

Mike Tyson's not all that bad. If you dig deep, dig real deep, go all the way to China, I'm sure you'll find there's a nice guy in there.
GEORGE FOREMAN

Me and Jake LaMotta grew up in the same neighbourhood. You wanna know how popular Jake was? When we played hide-and-seek, nobody ever looked for LaMotta.
ROCKY GRAZIANO

Don King doesn't care about black or white. He just cares about green.
LARRY HOLMES

Rocky Marciano couldn't carry my jockstrap.
LARRY HOLMES

Brian London possesses the most unbeautiful face – it looks as if it, at one time, fell apart and was reassembled by a drunken mechanic.
MICHAEL PARKINSON

He has turned defensive boxing into a poetic art. Trouble is, nobody ever knocked anybody out with a poem.
EDDIE SHAW, of Herol "Bomber" Graham

He has everything a boxer needs except speed, stamina, a punch, and ability to take punishment. In other words, he owns a pair of shorts.
BLACKIE SHERROD, of an unnamed contender

Cricket

He always appeared to be wearing a tumble-dried ferret on his top lip.
RICK BROADBENT, of Merv Hughes

The other advantage England have got when Phil Tufnell is bowling is that he isn't fielding.
IAN CHAPPELL

To dismiss this lad [Mike] Denness, you don't have to bowl fast, you just have to run up fast.
BRIAN CLOSE

It's difficult to be more laid-back than David Gower without being actually comatose.
FRANCES EDMONDS

Derek Randall bats like an octopus with piles.
MATTHEW ENGEL

Illy [Ray Illingworth] had the man-management skills of Basil Fawlty.
DARREN GOUGH

Does your husband play cricket as well?
MERV HUGHES, to Robin Smith

One of the few people capable of looking more dishevelled at the start of a six-hour century than at the end of it.
MARTIN JOHNSON, of Michael Atherton

[Angus] Fraser's approach to the wicket currently resembles someone who has his braces caught in the sightscreen.
MARTIN JOHNSON

At best, his action is suspicious. At worst it belongs in a darts tournament.
MICHAEL PARKINSON, of Muttiah Muralitharan

I suspect he [Andre Nel] has the IQ of an empty swimming pool.
ADAM PARORE

A fast bowler so hot-headed it was a surprise his sun hat never burst into flames.
HARRY PEARSON, of John Snow

Only his mother would describe him as an athlete.
DEREK PRINGLE, of Ashley Giles

W.G. Grace was by no conceivable standard a good man. He was a cheat on and off the cricket field.
C.P. SNOW

I've seen him playing football before a Test match, and believe me, his second touch was always a throw-in.
ALEC STEWART, of Shane Warne

Ian Botham couldn't bowl a hoop downhill.
FRED TRUEMAN

I know why he's bought a house by the sea – so that he'll be able to go for a walk on the water.
FRED TRUEMAN, of Geoffrey Boycott

There's only one head bigger than Tony Greig – and that's Birkenhead.
FRED TRUEMAN

Denis Compton was the only player to call his partner for a run and wish him good luck at the same time.
JOHN WARR

Kevin Pietersen would be deemed brash by a Texan assertiveness coach.
SIMON WILDE

Jason Gillespie is a thirty-year-old in a thirty-six-year-old body.
BOB WILLIS

ROD MARSH: So how's your wife and my kids?
IAN BOTHAM: The wife's fine, the kids are retarded.

SHANE WARNE: I've been waiting two years to humiliate you again.
DARYLL CULLINAN: Looks like you spent the time eating.

MARK WAUGH: What are you doing out here? There's no way you're good enough to play for England.
JAMES ORMOND: Maybe not, but at least I'm the best player in my family.

Golf

His divots go further than his drives.
ANON

He's got a swing like an octopus putting up a deckchair.
ANON

He's got a swing like a caveman killing his lunch.
ANON

Bob Hope has a beautiful short game. Unfortunately it's off the tee.
JIMMY DEMARET

The only time Nick Faldo opens his mouth is to change feet.
DAVID FEHERTY

Colin Montgomerie has a face like a warthog that has been stung by a wasp.
DAVID FEHERTY

Sammy Davis Jr hits the ball 130 yards and his jewellery goes 150.
BOB HOPE

There are over 150 golf courses in the Palm Springs area and Gerry Ford is never sure which one he's going to play until his second shot.
BOB HOPE

Whenever I play golf with Gerry Ford, I usually try to make it a foursome: Ford, me, a paramedic, and a faith healer.
BOB HOPE

Some of these legends have been around golf a long time. When they mention a good grip, they're talking about their dentures.
BOB HOPE

Hubert Green swings like a drunk trying to find a keyhole in the dark.
JIM MURRAY

You've just one problem: you stand too close to the ball – after you've hit it.
SAM SNEAD, to an unnamed golfer

Motor Racing

James Hunt, he's champion of the world, right? The problem is that he thinks he's the king of the goddam world as well.
MARIO ANDRETTI

Fast on his day. Otherwise he usually connects with the scenery.
ANON, of Andrea de Cesaris

Eddie Irvine is the classic case of the male inadequacy syndrome.
DAVID COULTHARD

The most selfish driver I have ever worked with. He was happy enough to choose me as a partner, but when he realised I could drive quickly our friendship changed. He saw me as a threat and he didn't like it.
JOHNNY HERBERT, of Michael Schumacher

He's brash and can be abrasive. He goads people. He's the Ian Paisley of Formula 1.
DAMON HILL, of Eddie Irvine

You never know what's going on in his head, and often he doesn't seem to know himself.
NIGEL MANSELL, of Nelson Piquet

I am a better and more courageous racer than he will be if he is in Formula 1 for a lifetime. He will be more of a chauffeur, making the car work for him.
NIGEL MANSELL, of Alain Prost

The Sao Paulo taxi driver.
NELSON PIQUET, of Ayrton Senna

He seems to be very moody and I find it hard to get on with moody people.
MICHAEL SCHUMACHER, of Damon Hill

He's always complaining. It is normal for him.
AYRTON SENNA, of Nigel Mansell

Ayrton Senna had an immense number of collisions. And they could not all have been everybody else's fault.
JACKIE STEWART

Rugby

Since when did a Welsh three-quarter wear a fake tan, spiked hair and silver boots?
ANON, of Gavin Henson

The Welsh team looked good on paper, but turned out to be not so good on grass.
ANON

I'd rather crawl across broken glass naked than speak to Will Carling.
DICK BEST

Fifty-seven old farts.
WILL CARLING, of the Rugby Football Union executive

A Mount Rushmore of a face.
GERALD DAVIES, of Martin Johnson

Clive [Woodward]'s coaching methods were something new to me and left me a bit bewildered.
GAVIN HENSON

He is just a child, just so incredibly immature.
NICK FARR-JONES, of Austin Healey

His shyness is derivative of not having a high intellect.
SCOTT GIBBS, of Gavin Henson

Austin Healey shows what a dwarf mind he possesses.
GREG GROWDEN

An ape, a plank, and a plod.
AUSTIN HEALEY, of Justin Harrison

I think Brian Moore's gnashers are the kind you get from a
DIY shop and hammer in yourself.
PAUL RANDALL

The winger resembles Mother Brown, running with a high
knee-lift and sometimes not progressing far from the spot
where he started.
MARK REASON, of Simon Geoghegan

Jack Rowell has the acerbic wit of Dorothy Parker and,
according to most New Zealanders, a similar knowledge of
rugby.
MARK REASON

He is a parasite who feeds off my career and it's time that
he got a life. How does he live with himself? How does it
feel to be a man with no friends in rugby?
WENDELL SAILOR, of David Campese

Rugby is a good occasion for keeping thirty bullies far from the centre of the city.
OSCAR WILDE

Soccer

All he does is lie on the treatment table twice a day.
DICK ADVOCAAT, of Rangers' Marco Negri

It is clear that [José] Mourinho believes he is superior to the rest and that his success has gone to his head.
MANUEL ALMUNIA

Alan Ball's voice is so high-pitched that only dogs can hear him.
ANON

Watching Peter Crouch in action is like seeing Bambi on ice.
ANON

Emile Heskey has the turning circle of a 747.
ANON

Dracula is more comfortable with crosses.
ANON, of goalkeeper David James

They call David James "Cinderella" because he is always late for the ball.
ANON

Mickey Quinn was to dieting what Brian Sewell is to army camouflage trousers.
ANON

If you needed somebody to take a penalty kick to save your life, Chris Waddle, with his hunched shoulders and lethargic air, would rank just below Long John Silver.
ANON

A teabag stays in the cup longer.
ANON, of Charlton

They've had to replace the new executive boxes at Nottingham Forest because they were facing the wrong way – they were facing the pitch!
ANON

Then his eyesight started to go and he took up refereeing.
ANON

I call him "The Crab" because he only plays sideways.
RON ATKINSON, of Ray Wilkins

Devon Loch was a better finisher.
RON ATKINSON, of Aston Villa

When God gave him this enormous footballing talent he took his brain out at the same time to equal it up.
TONY BANKS, of Paul Gascoigne

He's got the brains of a rocking-horse.
DAVE BASSETT, of Sheffield United goalkeeper Simon Tracey

The Sheffield United board have been loyal to me. When I came here they said there would be no money, and they've kept their promise.
DAVE BASSETT

There's more meat on a toothpick.
ALAN BIRCHENALL, of Robbie Savage

He's the moaningest minnie I've ever known.
JOHN BOND, of Kenny Dalglish

Johnan Cruyff isn't worthy of consideration as a coach. He thinks he's a diva.
JAVIER CLEMENTE

Trevor Brooking floats like a butterfly . . . and stings like one.
BRIAN CLOUGH

I told Eddie Gray that, with his injury record, if he'd been a racehorse they'd have had him shot.
BRIAN CLOUGH

He couldn't trap a landmine.
BRIAN CLOUGH, of Gary Megson

The only money Forest directors cough up is when they buy a golden goal ticket.
BRIAN CLOUGH

What's the point of giving you the ball when there's a genius [John Robertson] on the other wing?
BRIAN CLOUGH, to Martin O'Neill

Whenever I felt off-colour, I'd sit next to Robbo because then I looked like Errol Flynn.
BRIAN CLOUGH, of John Robertson

Football hooligans? Well, there are ninety-two club chairmen for a start.
BRIAN CLOUGH

An irascible fellow with a taste for amateur dramatics.
PATRICK COLLINS, of Neil Warnock

I doubt if Sven-Goran Eriksson has even heard of Ian Wright. If only the rest of us could say the same.
PATRICK COLLINS

For years I thought the club's name was Partick Thistle Nil.
BILLY CONNOLLY

Having seen him finish on a day-to-day basis, I would think his last hat-trick was at primary school.
STEVE COPPELL, of Bruce Dyer

John Barnes's problem is that he gets injured appearing on *A Question of Sport*.
TOMMY DOCHERTY

I wouldn't only not sign him, I wouldn't let him in the ground.
TOMMY DOCHERTY, of Vinnie Jones

He can't run, can't tackle and can't head a ball. The only time he goes forward is to toss the coin.
TOMMY DOCHERTY, of Ray Wilkins

Sport

There are three types of Oxo cubes. Light brown for chicken stock, dark brown for beef stock, and light blue for laughing stock.
TOMMY DOCHERTY, of Manchester City

We don't use a stopwatch to judge our golden goal competition now, we use a calendar.
TOMMY DOCHERTY, of Wolves

I just opened the trophy cabinet. Two Japanese prisoners of war came out.
TOMMY DOCHERTY, of Wolves

The ideal board of directors should be made up of three men: two dead and the other dying.
TOMMY DOCHERTY

After the match an official asked for two of my players to take a dope test. I offered him the referee.
TOMMY DOCHERTY

He needed five stitches – three in the first half and two at the interval when his brain started to seep through.
ALEX FERGUSON, of Steve Bruce

Part of the problem is, Eric [Cantona] can't tackle. He couldn't tackle a fish supper.
ALEX FERGUSON

He's come here from Japan and he's telling English people how to organise our football. He should keep his mouth firmly shut.
ALEX FERGUSON, of Arsène Wenger

Old vinegar face.
ALEX FERGUSON, of Arsène Wenger

Brian Clough's record speaks for itself . . . if it can get a word in.
CRIS FREDDI

He doesn't know a goal-line from a clothes-line.
BARRY FRY, of David Sullivan

He had a bandage on his head. Perhaps one of his eyelashes had fallen out.
GEORGE GRAHAM, of Tomas Brolin

As well as being England's first managerial turnip, Graham Taylor has prime ministerial qualities, combining the personality of John Major with the gift of prophecy of Neville Chamberlain.
STEVE GRANT

Old Sicknote should get a part on *Animal Hospital*.
JIMMY GREAVES, of Darren Anderton

Peter Beardsley is the only player who, when he appears on TV, [makes] Daleks hide behind the sofa.
NICK HANCOCK

The whine merchant.
MATT HUGHES, of Thierry Henry

We reckon he covers every blade of grass on the pitch – mainly because his first touch is terrible.
DAVID JONES, of Carlton Palmer

Sport

He scores goals in big games but the next minute he looks like a pub player.
MARK LAWRENSON, of Luis Garcia

The best two clubs in London are Stringfellow's and the Hippodrome.
TERRY McDERMOTT

His management style seems to be based on the chaos theory.
MARK McGHEE, of Barry Fry

Comparing [Paul] Gascoigne to Pelé is like comparing Rolf Harris to Rembrandt.
RODNEY MARSH

A mouthy serial delinquent.
DAVID MELLOR, of Craig Bellamy

Ricardo Carvalho seems to have problems understanding things. Maybe he should have an IQ test.
JOSÉ MOURINHO

I think he is one of these people who is a voyeur. He likes to watch other people. There are some guys who, when they are at home, have a big telescope to see what happens in other families. He speaks, speaks, speaks about Chelsea.
JOSÉ MOURINHO, of Arsène Wenger

They brought the bus and they left the bus in front of the goal.
JOSÉ MOURINHO, of Spurs' defensive tactics

A man capable of destroying the mirror because he didnae like the way the face in it was looking at him.
MATTHEW NORMAN, of Graeme Souness

José Mourinho recently turned down the post of Pope when he heard it was something in the way of an assistant position.
HARRY PEARSON

[John] Hartson's got more previous than Jack the Ripper.
HARRY REDKNAPP

[Arjen] Robben is a big actor and he did well enough to win an Oscar.
JOSÉ REINA

Kevin Keegan is not fit to lace George Best's drinks.
JOHN ROBERTS

With a record like his in management I would have kept quiet, yet he had the audacity to tell me how I should be doing my work.
BOBBY ROBSON, of Alan Ball

Daft as a brush.
BOBBY ROBSON, of Paul Gascoigne

[Pat] Crerand's deceptive – he's slower than you think.
BILL SHANKLY

If Everton were playing down at the bottom of my garden, I'd draw the curtains.
BILL SHANKLY

Sport

There are two great teams in Liverpool – Liverpool and Liverpool Reserves.
BILL SHANKLY

Matt [Busby] has got a bad back. I tell you it's two bad backs! And not much of a midfield either.
BILL SHANKLY, of Manchester United

Tommy Smith would start a riot in a graveyard.
BILL SHANKLY

After one game Barnsley wanted to sign him. After two they decided to send him back.
JIM SMITH, of Deon Burton

If Stan Bowles could pass a betting shop like he can pass a ball he'd have no worries at all.
ERNIE TAGG

Compared to my chairman at Southend, Ken Bates is Mary Poppins.
DAVID WEBB

Norman Hunter doesn't tackle opponents so much as break them down for resale as scrap.
JULIE WELCH

A basketball player.
ARSÈNE WENGER, of Peter Crouch

When you give success to stupid people, it makes them more stupid sometimes and not more intelligent.
ARSÈNE WENGER, of José Mourinho

If the way to play the game is not to play, then I will stay at home and read a book. ARSÈNE WENGER, of Chelsea

A player with a heart the size of a diamond ear-stud. RICHARD WILLIAMS, of Harry Kewell

The man's like a wet fish. He's got as much passion as a tadpole.
IAN WRIGHT, of Sven-Goran Eriksson

The referee was booking everyone. I thought he was filling in his lottery numbers.
IAN WRIGHT

Tennis

The baseball cap worn back to front makes him resemble a redneck petrol pump attendant.
ANON, of Lleyton Hewitt

In her leather-appliquéd skirts and 70s wire-rim eyeglasses, she's the "Tootsie" of tennis.
MR BLACKWELL, of Martina Navratilova

A walking, talking, screaming, squawking metaphor for What's Wrong With Young People Today.
JULIE BURCHILL, of John McEnroe

Lindsay Davenport has the turning circle of a station wagon.
MIKE DICKSON

Sport

Like a Volvo, Björn Borg is rugged, has good after-sales service, and is very dull.
CLIVE JAMES

As charming as a dead mouse in a loaf of bread.
CLIVE JAMES, of John McEnroe

Hair like badly turned broccoli.
CLIVE JAMES, of John McEnroe

Ilie Nastase is a Hamlet who wants to play a clown, but he is no good at it; his gags are bad, his timing is terrible and he never knows how he's going over the top – which last drawback is the kiss of death for a comic.
CLIVE JAMES

Maria Sharapova has lived so long in Florida that she sounds like one of those high-octane weather girls for CNN.
MARTIN JOHNSON

Did you win a lottery to be linesman?
JOHN MCENROE

She sounds like a live pig being slaughtered.
FREW MACMILLAN, of Maria Sharapova's grunts

Imagine the love child of Jimmy Connors and the young Mike Tyson.
MATTHEW NORMAN, of Lleyton Hewitt

Michael Chang has all the fire and passion of a public service announcement.
ALEX RAMSEY

159

Tim Henman must be the least charismatic person in the history of sport.
ARTHUR SMITH

He's like a human form of beige.
LINDA SMITH, of Tim Henman

Others

Ellen MacArthur could moan for England.
ANON

He has so many fish hooks in his nose, he looks like a piece of bait.
BOB COSTAS, on the nose piercings of basketball player Dennis Rodman

Two-piece snooker cues are popular these days, but Alex Higgins doesn't use one because there aren't any instructions.
STEVE DAVIS

Snooker player Stephen Hendry is the only man with a face that comes with free garlic bread.
NICK HANCOCK

I remember when Steve Davis used to take Valium as a stimulant.
DENNIS TAYLOR

Seb [Coe] is a Yorkshireman. So he's a complete bastard and will do well in politics.
DALEY THOMPSON

Basketball player George McGinnis has got the body of a Greek god and the running ability of a Greek goddess.
DICK VITALE

His natural expression is that of a man who may have mislaid his winning lottery ticket.
PAUL WEAVER, of snooker player Matthew Stevens

I wouldn't be surprised if one day Carl [Lewis]'s halo slipped and choked him.
ALLAN WELLS

The Stage

Darling, they've absolutely ruined your perfectly dreadful play.
TALLULAH BANKHEAD, to Tennessee Williams after seeing the film version of one of his plays

If you really want to help the American theatre, darling, be an audience.
TALLULAH BANKHEAD, to a young actress

I see no future for A.A. Milne, whose plots are as thin as a filleted anchovy.
H. DENNIS BRADLEY

Your characters talk like typewriting and you yourself talk like a telegram.
MRS PATRICK CAMPBELL, to Noël Coward

Andrew Lloyd Webber was born with a face like a melted Wellington boot.
JEREMY CLARKSON

The Stage

My dear chap! Good isn't the word!
W.S. GILBERT, to an actor who had given a poor performance

The problem with [Andrew] Lloyd Webber's music is not that it sounds as if it were written by other composers, but that it sounds as if it were written by Lloyd Webber.
GERALD KAUFMAN

A brassy, brazened witch on a mortgaged broomstick.
WALTER KERR, of Ethel Merman

I always said I'd like [Lionel] Barrymore's acting till the cows came home. Well, ladies and gentlemen, last night the cows came home.
GEORGE J. NATHAN

To me, Edith [Evans] looks like something that would eat its young.
DOROTHY PARKER

Sarah Brightman couldn't act scared on the New York subway at four o'clock in the morning.
JOEL SEGAL

You are my fifth favourite actor, the first four being the Marx Brothers.
GEORGE BERNARD SHAW, to Cedric Hardwicke

It is a consolation to know that such an artist as Madame [Sarah] Bernhardt has not only worn that yellow, ugly dress, but has been photographed in it.
OSCAR WILDE

An ego like a raging tooth.
W.B. YEATS, of Mrs Patrick Campbell

Cutting Critics

Mr Webster Booth and Miss Anne Ziegler sing delightfully and very, very often.
JAMES AGATE, of *Sweet Yesterday*

Farley Granger played Mr Darcy with all the flexibility of a telegraph pole.
BROOKS ATKINSON

When Mr Wilbur calls his play *Halfway to Hell* he under-estimates the distance.
BROOKS ATKINSON

Annette Crosbie played Viola like a Shetland pony.
ANON, of *Twelfth Night*

There is less in this than meets the eye.
TALLULAH BANKHEAD, of *Aglavaine and Selsyette*

Perfectly Scandalous was one of those plays in which all the actors, unfortunately, enunciated very clearly.
ROBERT BENCHLEY

For those who missed it the first time, this is your golden opportunity: you can miss it again.
MICHAEL BILLINGTON, of the revival of *Godspell*

It opened at 8.40 sharp and closed at 10.40 dull.
HEYWOOD C. BROUN

Lillian Gish comes on stage as if she'd been sent for to sew rings on the new curtains.
MRS PATRICK CAMPBELL

The only moving thing about Charlton Heston's performance was his wig.
MICHAEL COVENEY

I never realised before that Albert married beneath him.
NOËL COWARD, after seeing Anna Neagle play Queen Victoria in *The Glorious Years*

Just as long as the real thing and twice as noisy.
NOËL COWARD, of Lionel Bart's World War Two musical *Blitz!*

Two things should be cut: the second act and the child's throat.
NOËL COWARD

Must be seen to be depreciated.
ROBERT GARLAND, of *Victory Belles*

Cedric Hardwicke conducted the soul-selling transaction with the thoughtful dignity of a grocer selling a pound of cheese.
HUBERT GRIFFITH, of *Dr Faustus*

I have knocked everything in this play except the chorus girls' knees, and there God anticipated me.
PERCY HAMMOND

I don't like the play, but then I saw it under adverse conditions – the curtain was up.
GEORGE S. KAUFMAN

The only way this actress will get her name into the *New York Times* is if somebody shoots her.
GEORGE S. KAUFMAN

I have seen stronger plots in a cemetery.
STEWART KLEIN, of *Break a Leg*

This pitiful little thing has to do with horse racing, and you might perhaps say that it is by Imbecility out of Staggering Incompetence.
BERNARD LEVIN, of *Dazzling Prospect*

I shall content myself with saying that its best tune, the already famous "Don't Cry For Me, Argentina", is inferior as a melody to the ones I used when a boy to hear improvised on a saxophone outside the Albert Hall by a busker with only three fingers on his left hand.
BERNARD LEVIN, of *Evita*

A pretty fellow whom the moving pictures should exultantly capture without delay, if they have any respect for the dramatic stage.
GEORGE JEAN NATHAN, of Charlton Heston in *Design for a Stained Glass Window*

Miss [Kay] Strozzi had the temerity to wear as truly horrible a gown as ever I have seen on the American stage ... Had she not luckily been strangled by a member of the cast while disporting this garment, I should have fought my way to the stage and done her in myself.
DOROTHY PARKER, of *The Silent Witness*

If you don't knit, bring a good book.
DOROTHY PARKER

The House Beautiful is play lousy.
DOROTHY PARKER

This wasn't just plain terrible, this was fancy terrible, this was terrible with raisins in it.
DOROTHY PARKER

A suite of temper tantrums all amplified to a piercing pitch that would not be out of place in a musical about one of chess's somewhat noisier fellow sports, like stock-car racing.
FRANK RICH, of *Chess*

Starlight Express is the perfect gift for the kid who has everything except parents.
FRANK RICH

It is greatly to Mrs Patrick Campbell's credit that, bad as the play was, her acting was worse.
GEORGE BERNARD SHAW, of *Fedora*

There was a heated diversion of opinion in the lobbies during the interval but a small conservative majority took the view that it might be as well to remain in the theatre.
KENNETH TYNAN, of *The Glorious Days*

It's ominous when an audience leave a musical whistling the scenery.
VARIETY, of *Twentieth Century*

I've seen more excitement at the opening of an umbrella.
EARL WILSON

Most of the heroes are in the audience.
WALTER WINCHELL, of *The Hero in Man*

The scenery was beautiful, but the actors got in front of it.
ALEXANDER WOOLLCOTT

Random Insults

Personality

I have had a perfectly wonderful evening, but this wasn't it.
GROUCHO MARX

Any similarity between him and a human being is purely coincidental.

He's depriving a village somewhere of its idiot.

Before he came along we were hungry. Now we are fed up.

At least he's not obnoxious like so many other people – he's obnoxious in different and worse ways!

Talking to him is about as interesting as watching a scab form.

He was a solemn, unsmiling, sanctimonious old iceberg who looked like he was waiting for a vacancy in the Trinity.
MARK TWAIN

He has delusions of adequacy.

171

He's so mean that when he takes a £5 note from his wallet, the Queen blinks in the light.

Anyone who told him to be himself couldn't have given him worse advice.

The higher a monkey climbs, the more you see of its behind.
JOSEPH STILWELL

He could start a fight in an empty room.

He would be out of his depth in a puddle.

She's the original good time that was had by all.
BETTE DAVIS

She's happy to paint the town red with any man with a full wallet and she's happy to give him the brush when it's empty.

When they made him they broke the mould but some of it grew back.

People take an instant dislike to him because it saves time.

We all sprang from the apes but he didn't spring far enough.

Do you think I can buy back my introduction to you?
GROUCHO MARX

He could be described as charming, intelligent and witty. And perhaps one day he will be.

Personality

He is so boring he can't even entertain a doubt.

He's so far up himself he's in danger of turning inside out.

Like a cushion, he always bore the impress of the last man who had sat on him.

Fine words! I wonder where you stole them.
JONATHAN SWIFT

He's a difficult man to forget. But it's definitely worth the effort.

He's a man of hidden talents – and as soon as we find one we'll let you know.

He was so unpopular that he even had to organise his own surprise birthday party.

Dancing with her was like moving a piano.
RING LARDNER

His father looks on him as the son he never had.

His table manners give vultures a bad name.

The last time I saw him he was walking down Lovers' Lane holding his own hand.
FRED ALLEN

He has all the characteristics of a dog except loyalty.

He couldn't organise a piss-up in a brewery.

173

He was as great as a man can be without morality.
ALEXIS DE TOCQUEVILLE

He's as devious as a bag of weasels.

He has an inferiority complex, but not a very good one.

Like acting with 210 pounds of condemned veal.
CORAL BROWNE

Ordinarily people live and learn – he just lives.

He's as fake as a three-dollar bill.

She'll tolerate any man who doesn't fit the bill, provided that he foots it.

He is so in touch with his feminine side, they are practically dating.

Gee, what a terrific party. Later on we'll get some fluid and embalm each other.
NEIL SIMON

He is so slow that moss grows on him.

The only skill he has ever developed is the art of being obnoxious.

He was as useful in a crisis as a sheep.
DOROTHY EDEN

He's the kind of bore who's here today and here tomorrow.

Personality

He displays the tact and sensitivity of a rampaging bull elephant.

Everyone is gifted: some just open the package sooner.

She's been engaged more times than a telephone switch-board.

He's so greedy that when he goes to an "all you can eat" buffet, they have to install speed bumps.

I didn't attend the funeral, but I sent a nice letter saying I approved of it.
MARK TWAIN

Women fall at his feet – but only because of his breath.

He doesn't know the meaning of the word "failure", but then again he doesn't know the meaning of most words.

He doesn't just hold a conversation, he strangles it.

We don't have to put up with your snidey remarks, your total slobbiness, your socks that set off the sprinkler system.
RED DWARF

I've seen better arguments in a bowl of alphabet soup.

I've seen glaciers move faster than him.

He has all the maturity of wine bottled yesterday.

I could dance with you until the cows come home. On second thoughts, I'd rather dance with the cows until you come home.
GROUCHO MARX

He is so narrow-minded, he can see through a keyhole with both eyes.

He was in a class of his own, but only because none of the other boys would sit near him.

He would stab his best friend for the sake of writing an epigram on his tombstone.
OSCAR WILDE

He should do some soul-searching. Maybe he'll find one.

Never mind about running a company, you wouldn't trust him to run a bath.

He has done for this firm what King Herod did for babysitting.

He has a great deal of pride, but precious little to be proud of.

They don't make them like him any more, and for that we are truly grateful.

He is the same old sausage, fizzing and sputtering in his own grease.
HENRY JAMES

Personality

You couldn't find his personality with SatNav.

He has turned incompetence into an art form.

There goes a woman who knows all the things that can be taught and none of the things that cannot be taught.
COCO CHANEL

She has been married so many times that her marriage licence says "to whom it may concern".

Kiss her under the mistletoe? I wouldn't kiss her under an anaesthetic.

He'll doublecross that bridge when he comes to it.

The smaller the pip, the louder the squeak.

If they can make penicillin out of mouldy bread, they can sure make something out of you.
MUHAMMAD ALI

He says he will be boss of the company one day – and I think one day will be long enough.

He's got more neck than a giraffe.

He's so mean that when he opens his wallet, he has to fight off the moths.

He was a bit like a corkscrew. Twisted, cold and sharp.
KATE CRUISE O'BRIEN

He's like a windscreen wiper – wet, flaccid, moving from side to side, and bowing and scraping when you look at him.

He may have a slick mind, but it's given him an oily tongue.

He's the most overrated human being since Judas Iscariot won the AD 31 Best Disciple Competition.
BLACKADDER

The less he knows on any subject, the more stubbornly he knows it.

He seems to have had a charisma bypass operation.

He likes to tell you he's positive, but really he's just wrong at the top of his voice.

Like a death at a birthday party, you ruin all the fun.

Like a sucked and spat-out Smartie, you're no use to anyone.
JOHN COOPER CLARKE

He used to be fairly indecisive, but now he's not so certain.

He has the energy and drive of a snail on valium.

His mother should have thrown him away and kept the stork.
MAE WEST

Personality

You could fit all his friends into a phone box.

She never learned to swim, simply because she couldn't keep her mouth shut for that long.

He always tries to do the right thing, but only after he's tried everything else.

His men would follow him anywhere but only out of morbid curiosity.

He is an old bore. Even the grave yawns for him.
HERBERT BEERBOHM TREE

He never opens his mouth without subtracting from the sum of human knowledge.

He has all the charisma of a magnum of chloroform.

He trod on a snail the other day because it was following him around; there were two, but the other one ran off before he could catch it.

He is not only dull himself, he is the cause of dullness in others.
SAMUEL JOHNSON

Being told you have his full support and backing is rather like being measured by an undertaker.

She is such a bad cook that she uses the smoke alarm as a timer.

She is such a bad cook that when she throws a dinner party, the local fire brigade cancel all leave.

She is such a bad cook that dinner guests cheer if the gravy moves.

She is such a bad cook that her pie-filling bubbles over and eats the enamel off the bottom of the oven.

She is such a bad cook that her two best recipes are meatloaf and apple pie, but her dinner guests can't tell which is which.

She is such a bad cook that her dog goes to the neighbours' house to eat.

She is such a bad cook that her family pray *after* they eat.

She has the sort of charm that rubs off with tissues and cold cream.

He is so mean, he won't let his baby have more than one measle at a time.

He made enemies as naturally as soap makes suds.
PERCIVAL WILDE

He is as good as his word – and his word is no good.

Under no circumstances should he be allowed to breed.

Personality

He was so crooked, you could have used his spine for a safety-pin.
DOROTHY L. SAYERS

Her house is so dirty that she has to wipe her feet before going outside.

He's the sort of guy who gives failures a bad name.

He is a well-balanced individual – he has a chip on each shoulder.

His existence has yet to create the slightest ripple on the millpond of achievement.

I have nothing but confidence in you. And very little of that.
GROUCHO MARX

They remind me of a public toilet – she's engaged and he's vacant.

She's about as cuddly as a snarling pit-bull.

He's the kind of man who picks his friends – to pieces.
MAE WEST

He will never be able to live down to his reputation.

I lost closer friends than "darling Georgie" the last time I was deloused.
BLACKADDER

His family tree is good but he is the sap.

He's so greedy that his cereal bowl comes complete with a lifeguard.

He's the sort of self-made man that can't resist passing on the recipe.

He has Van Gogh's ear for music.

He's got a mouth on him like the Channel Tunnel.

He stands firmly on both feet in mid-air on both sides of an issue.
HOMER FERGUSSON

She has been married so many times she has a season ticket for the registry office.

He was like a cock who thought the sun had risen to hear him crow.
GEORGE ELIOT

He is living proof that practice does not make perfect.

He not only overflowed with learning, but stood in the slop.
SYDNEY SMITH

The only place he's ever invited is outside.

Anyone who ever extends him the hand of friendship is likely to lose a couple of fingers.

Personality

If all the girls attending the Yale prom were laid end to end, I wouldn't be at all surprised.
DOROTHY PARKER

Success has definitely turned his head. It's just a pity it didn't finish the job and wring his neck.

They say he plays football like Rooney . . . Mickey Rooney.

You take the lies out of him, and he'll shrink to the size of your hat; you take the malice out of him, and he'll disappear.
MARK TWAIN

He has a difficulty for every solution.

His talent would be indiscernible, even under a microscope.

He may not have many faults but he certainly makes the most of the ones he has.

He is a man of splendid abilities but utterly corrupt. He shines and stinks like rotten mackerel by moonlight.
JOHN RANDOLPH

He's a mouse studying to be a rat.

If she holds her nose any higher she'll develop a double chin at the back of her neck.

Failure has gone to his head.

And I want to thank you for all the enjoyment you've taken out of it.
GROUCHO MARX

They say she's got a promising voice; perhaps she'll take notice and promise to stop singing.

He's about as welcome as a fox in a henhouse.

Debating against him is no fun. Say something insulting and he looks at you like a whipped dog.
HAROLD WILSON

She's a treasure. Who dug her up?

I could never learn to like her, except on a raft at sea with no other provisions in sight.
MARK TWAIN

He's a man of hidden shallows.

He doesn't have ulcers, but he's a carrier.

He has a knack of making strangers immediately.

He has sat on the fence so long that iron his entered his soul.
DAVID LLOYD GEORGE

He's down to earth – but not quite far enough.

If you see two people talking and one looks bored, he's the other one.

Personality

Every time I look at you I get a fierce desire to be lonesome.
OSCAR LEVANT

His mouth is getting too big for his muzzle.

I don't like her. But don't misunderstand me: my dislike is purely platonic.
HERBERT BEERBOHM TREE

She is the kind of woman who climbed the ladder of success – wrong by wrong.
MAE WEST

He has only two temperamental outbursts a year – each lasts six months.

I'll never forget the first time we met – although I keep trying.

Some cause happiness wherever they go; others whenever they go.
OSCAR WILDE

Some people are one in a million – he was won in a raffle.

When they made him they kept the mould and threw him away.

He is a fine friend. He stabs you in the front.
LEONARD LOUIS LEVINSON

He's a prime candidate for natural deselection.

Random Insults

Some people stay longer in an hour than others can in a week.
WILLIAM DEAN HOWELLS

It's hard to believe he beat a million other sperm.

He's not man enough to pull on stretch socks.

Some people are has-beens. He's a never-was.

She tells enough white lies to ice a cake.
MARGOT ASQUITH

He's about as much use as a chocolate teapot.

He's about as much use as an ashtray on a motorcycle.

He's about as much use as a glass hammer.

He's about as much use as a carpet fitter's ladder.

I have a mind to join a club and beat you over the head with it.
GROUCHO MARX

He's about as much use as a lead parachute.

He's about as much use as a can of dinosaur repellent.

He got into the gene pool while the lifeguard wasn't looking.

Personality

Why are we honouring this man? Have we run out of human beings?
MILTON BERLE

He's been compared to many great men. Unfavourably. But he has been compared to them.

He's just visiting this planet.

He was so crooked that when he died they had to screw him into the ground.
BOB HOPE

And there he was: reigning supreme at number two.

If he moved any slower, he'd rust.

I know she's outspoken, but by whom?
DOROTHY PARKER

She's got such a narrow mind, when she walks fast her earrings bang together.

He always has his ear to the ground – but only because he lives in the gutter.

He has all the virtues I dislike and none of the vices I admire.
WINSTON CHURCHILL

He often behaves like he has a tiger in the tank, but the trouble is there is a donkey at the wheel.

He's acquitting himself in a way that no jury ever would.

He grows on people – like a wart.

He has a speech impediment – his foot.

I have never killed a man, but I have read many obituaries with great pleasure.
CLARENCE DARROW

He's a self-made man, and it's good of him to take the blame.

He is brilliant to the top of his boots.
DAVID LLOYD GEORGE

His personality is split so many ways he goes alone for group therapy.

He's not only a bachelor, he's the son of a bachelor.

He has left his body to science and science is contesting the will.
DAVID FROST

He has a lot of well-wishers – they'd all like to throw him down one.

He never chooses an opinion; he just wears whatever happens to be in style.
LEO TOLSTOY

Personality

He thinks by infection, catching an opinion like a cold.
JOHN RUSKIN

He is connected to the Police Department – by a pair of handcuffs.

A woman's mind is cleaner than a man's. She changes it more often.
OLIVER HERFORD

There's nothing wrong with him that reincarnation couldn't cure.

He's living proof that manure can grow legs and walk.

She looks at the world through green-coloured glasses.
SONIA MASELLO

He has reached rock bottom and started to dig.

He always thinks twice before saying nothing.

I like long walks, especially when they are taken by people who annoy me.
FRED ALLEN

You know I could rent you out as a decoy for duck hunters?
GROUCHO MARX

They said he was an asset. They were two letters out.

She's as tough as an ox. When she dies she'll be turned into Bovril.
DOROTHY PARKER

He's as useless as rubber lips on a woodpecker.

When he talks he reminds me of Moses – every time he opens his mouth the bull rushes.
ROBERT ORBEN

The only regular exercise he gets is stretching the truth.

He always enters a room voice first.

He wouldn't spot a good idea if one ran up to him, waving and shouting, "Hi, I'm a good idea."

She had a pretty gift for quotation, which is a serviceable substitute for wit.
W. SOMERSET MAUGHAM

He fills a much-needed gap.

He can compress the most words into the smallest idea of any man I know.
ABRAHAM LINCOLN

He's got more front than Blackpool.

He has always been conceited. When he was young he joined the Navy so the world could see him.

I've seen more articulate lorries.

Personality

She has the answer to everything and the solution to nothing.
OSCAR LEVANT

If his conscience could be surgically removed, it would be a minor operation.

She proceeds to dip her little fountain-pen filler into pots of oily venom and to squirt the mixture at all her friends.
HAROLD NICOLSON

He's always in the right place, but at the wrong time.

The only big thing about him is his opinion of himself.

Some men are born mediocre, some men achieve mediocrity, and some men have mediocrity thrust upon them.
JOSEPH HELLER

His personality is infectious – but then so was the bubonic plague.

He'd steal the straw from his mother's kennel.

He's got more issues than *National Geographic*.

I regard you with an indifference bordering on aversion.
ROBERT LOUIS STEVENSON

He is wetter than a halibut's bathing costume.

He's the sort of man you could lose in a crowd of two.

He has no more sense of direction than a bunch of firecrackers.

He's such a snob he has an unlisted postcode.

He ought to be a member of the Parole Board because he never lets anyone finish a sentence.

He's so two-faced I bet he doesn't know which one to wash in the morning.

She makes it a rule never to repeat gossip: there's no need to, she always starts it.

Some people say he's superficial – but that's just on the surface.

He has a concrete mind – permanently set.

You only have to listen to him for a minute or two to realise why he's got such a wide circle of nodding acquaintances.

He should go far – the sooner the better!

She is such a good friend that she would throw all her acquaintances into the water for the pleasure of fishing them out again.
CHARLES TALLEYRAND

He has nothing to say but you have to listen a long time to discover that.

He doesn't listen to his conscience because he won't take advice from a complete stranger.

I'd like to buy her something to put around her neck – a rope perhaps?

That woman speaks eight languages and can't say "no" in any of them.
DOROTHY PARKER

The only thing that's cultured about her are her pearls.

The finest woman that ever walked the streets.
MAE WEST

She's not so much overdressed as wrapped up in herself.

She's been on more laps than a napkin.
WALTER WINCHELL

She has the knack of staying longer in a couple of hours than most people do in a couple of weeks.

I have a soft spot for her – a swamp at the bottom of my garden.

She has been kissed as often as a police-court Bible, and by much the same class of people.
ROBERTSON DAVIES

She did not so much cook food as assassinate it.

The trouble with him is that he's forgotten but not gone.

Give him two glasses and he'll make a spectacle of himself.

He's so slow he'd have to speed up to stop.

There's nothing wrong with you that couldn't be cured with a little Prozac and a polo mallet.
WOODY ALLEN

He puts the "suck" into success.

His tongue works so fast he could whisk an egg with it.

He doesn't realise that there are enough people to hate in the world already without his working so hard to give us another.

It only takes one drink to get him going, but he's not sure whether it's the eleventh or the twelfth.

You call that dancing? I've seen people on fire move better than that!
RED DWARF

If he blows his own trumpet much louder he won't have any breath left to call the tune.

He's so boring his dreams have muzak.

He's in touch with reality but it's a bad connection.

His shallowness was as sparkling as the surface of a rivulet.
MARY BRADDON

The trouble with her is that she lacks the power of conversation but not the power of speech.
GEORGE BERNARD SHAW

If she was cast as Lady Godiva, the horse would steal the show.

When he talks, other people get hoarse just listening.

When there's no more to be said on a subject, you can be certain he'll still be saying it.

He's a renewable energy source for hot-air balloons.

He's not the sort of man to trespass on your time – he encroaches on eternity.

He's not the worst person in the world, but until a worse one comes along, he'll do.

She's terribly class-conscious. She hasn't any class and everyone's conscious of it.

His approach is about as subtle as a pneumatic drill.

His vocabulary may not amount to much but it certainly has a fast turnover.

An evening with him is only marginally more enjoyable than being slapped repeatedly around the face with a wet haddock.

He always manages to keep his neck above water: you can tell from the colour of it.

He has a good family tree, but the crop is a failure.

He hasn't an enemy in the world, but all his friends hate him.

He'd make a lovely corpse.
CHARLES DICKENS

His origins are so low, you'd have to limbo under his family tree.

She had a voice like a drowned sailor. It died at C.

As far as he's concerned, refinement is a matter of knowing which fingers to use when you whistle for service.

His only purpose in life is to serve as a warning to others.

He's completely unspoiled by failure.
NOËL COWARD

I worship the ground he is buried in.

He's about as much fun as a wet weekend in Scunthorpe.

He's a good example of why some animals eat their young.

She could carry off anything; and some people said that she did.
ADA LEVERSON

If her nose was turned up any more, she'd blow her hat off every time she sneezed.

The reason he is so easily rattled is because he has a screw loose.

She plunged into a sea of platitudes, and with the powerful breaststroke of a Channel swimmer, made her confident way towards the white cliffs of the obvious.
W. SOMERSET MAUGHAM

He's as welcome as a rattlesnake at a square dance.

Remember, men, we're fighting for this woman's honour, which is probably more than she ever did.
GROUCHO MARX

Stupidity

He may look like an idiot and talk like an idiot but don't let that fool you. He really is an idiot.
GROUCHO MARX

If he were any more stupid, he'd have to be watered twice a week.

He has a room-temperature IQ.

He let his mind wander – and it hasn't come back yet.

He was born stupid, and greatly increased his birthright.
SAMUEL BUTLER

He has two brains: one is lost, the other is out looking for it.

He took an IQ test – and the results were negative.

Thinking isn't your strong suit, is it?
LOST IN SPACE

Stupidity

He's a gross ignoramus – 144 times worse than an ordinary ignoramus.

If he ever had a good idea, it would be beginner's luck.

One day he stopped to think and then forgot to start again.

He has been seen tossing breadcrumbs to helicopters.

If men were dominoes, he'd be the double-blank.
P.G. WODEHOUSE

His heart is in the right place, but I'm not sure about his brain.

If brains were chocolate, he wouldn't have enough to fill an M&M.

If brains were lard, he couldn't grease a frying pan.

If brains were bird droppings, he'd have a clean cage.

If brains were leather, he couldn't saddle a flea.

If brains were dynamite, he wouldn't have enough to blow his nose.

If brains were rain, he'd be a desert.

If brains were petrol, he wouldn't have enough to drive a Dinky Toy.

If brains were looks, he'd be the Elephant Man.

Why don't you bore a hole in yourself and let the sap run out?
GROUCHO MARX

He's at his wits' end, and it wasn't a long journey.

He's as bright as Alaska in December.

You've got the brain of a cheese sandwich.
RED DWARF

He says he's got a mind of his own, but it seems to operate on a timeshare principle.

So much goes over his head, he should be a limbo dancer.

He is useless on top of the ground; he ought to be under it, inspiring the cabbages.
MARK TWAIN

He's so dense that light bends around him.

He'd entertain a new thought as if it were his mother-in-law.

He can't count beyond ten with his shoes on.

If his IQ were two points higher, he'd be a rock.

How often the gods endow a man with a perfect profile and no brains to live up to it.
KATHERINE MANSFIELD

He's so dumb that he stopped making ice cubes because he forgot the recipe.

Even if he had a brain, he'd probably take it out and play with it.

He's as big as a gorilla and as strong as a gorilla. If he were as smart as a gorilla, he'd be fine.
SAM BAILEY

He's a miracle of nature: he has an IQ of two, yet he's still able to speak.

He's so dumb he used to stand in front of the mirror with his eyes closed so that he could see what he looked like asleep.

Your head is as empty as a hermit's address book.
BLACKADDER

He must have a large brain to hold so much ignorance.

He's as strong as an ox, and almost as intelligent.

He's so dumb he couldn't even pass a blood test.

He always speaks his mind, so usually he's silent.

A brain of feathers and a heart of lead.
ALEXANDER POPE

He has a mechanical mind – it's a shame he forgot to wind it up this morning.

He has a mind like a steel trap – always closed.

He's so dumb he threw breadcrumbs in the toilet to feed the toilet duck.

He's so dumb he threw a rock at the ground and missed.

The sum total of his knowledge could be written on the back of a postage stamp.

Nobody says he is dumb. They just say he was sixteen years old before he learned how to wave goodbye.

He doesn't have two brain cells to rub together.

His open mind should be closed for repairs.

Your brain's so minute, Baldrick, that if a hungry cannibal cracked your head open, there wouldn't be enough to cover a small water biscuit.
BLACKADDER

You couldn't find his IQ with a flashlight.

He's proof that evolution *can* go in reverse.

His main stumbling block is the one in his head.

He's lost his marble.

If stupidity were a crime, he would be number one on the Most Wanted list.

Stupidity

A mental midget with the IQ of a fence post.
TOM WAITS

He's an example of how the dinosaurs survived for millions of years with walnut-sized brains.

He was in line for brains, but he thought they said "pains", so he said, "No thanks."

I'm alone in space with a man who'd lose a battle of wits with a stuffed iguana.
RED DWARF

He has taken stupidity to new heights.

They put brighter heads than his on matchsticks.

He checked out of Hotel Brainy years ago.

He is a man of few words and doesn't know what either of them means.

His mind works like lightning – one brilliant flash and it's gone.

If he had half a mind to do anything, it would be a considerable improvement.

He knows so little and knows it so fluently.
ELLEN GLASGOW

Whatever anyone says to him goes in one ear and out the other because there is nothing blocking traffic.

He has the attention span of an overripe grapefruit.

He's got a marvellous substitute for his lack of brains – it's called silence.

People say he is the perfect idiot. I say that he's not perfect, but he is doing all right.

Some folks are wise and some are otherwise.
TOBIAS GEORGE SMOLLETT

He's so dumb that he sits on the TV and watches the sofa.

It would take him five minutes to boil a three-minute egg.

He's so stupid he got hit by a parked car.

You are last in God's great chain, unless there's an earwig around here you'd like to victimise.
BLACKADDER

Brains aren't everything – in fact in his case they're nothing.

Guillotining him would only make an aesthetic difference.

He's always lost in thought – it's unfamiliar territory.

Anything preying on his mind would starve to death.

Stupidity

He has the intellectual capacity of the average amoeba.

He ought to have a "This Space To Let" sign on his forehead.

He is so stupid you can't trust him with an idea.
JOHN STEINBECK

If you stand close enough to him, you can hear the ocean.

His mouth is in gear but his brain is in neutral.

He doesn't have the brain power to toast a crouton.

Fog rolled in the day he was born and a bit of it never rolled out.

His IQ is lower than a snake's belly.

He has a pulse, but that's about all.

His brain was sold separately and they were out of stock.

Some folks seem to have descended from the chimpanzee later than others.
KIN HUBBARD

He's the kind of man you would use as a blueprint to build an idiot.

The closest he'll ever get to a brainstorm is a slight drizzle.

His head whistles in a crosswind.

His mouth is working overtime, but his mind is on vacation.

He's immune from any serious head injury.

Some people don't hesitate to speak their minds because they have nothing to lose.

He is so slow that he takes an hour and a half to watch *Sixty Minutes*.

Had his brain been constructed of silk, he would have been hard-pressed to find the material to make a canary a set of cami-knickers.
P.G. WODEHOUSE

If he was any slower, he'd be in reverse.

He's about as sharp as a beachball.

He's about as smart as bait.

He's so dumb he once put a stamp on a fax.

He's so dumb the only thing he got on his IQ test was drool.

In the land of the witless, the half-wit is king.

Sometimes he can even think without moving his lips.

Ignorance can be cured, stupid is for ever.

Stupidity

If a fool and his money are easily parted, he must be bankrupt.

Ordinarily he is insane. But he has lucid moments when he is only stupid.
HEINRICH HEINE

When you look into his eyes, the only thing you can see is the back of his head.

He couldn't tell which way the elevator was going if he had two guesses.

He is living proof that man can live without a brain.

If ignorance is bliss, he must be the happiest person alive.

He's too pointless even to be called a pinhead.

A sharp tongue is no indication of a keen mind.

The eyes are open, the mouth moves, but Mr Brain has long since departed.
BLACKADDER

He had a brain transplant, but the brain rejected *him*.

His mind is so open that ideas simply pass through it.

He was born ignorant and has been losing ground ever since.

His brain is as good as new – simply because it's never been used.

He's so open-minded his brains have fallen out.

The twinkle in his eyes is actually the sun shining between his ears.

He forgot to pay his brain bill.

He's afraid he'll void his warranty if he thinks too much.

He has the IQ of belly-button fluff.

Some drink from the fountain of knowledge – he just gargled.

His ignorance covers the whole world like a blanket, and there's scarcely a hole in it anywhere.
MARK TWAIN

If intelligence were rain, he'd be holding an umbrella.

If you gave him a penny for his thoughts, you'd get change.

I don't know what makes him so stupid, but it really works.

You've got the brain of a four-year-old boy, and I'll bet he was glad to get rid of it.
GROUCHO MARX

He's a person of rare intelligence – it's rare when he shows any.

Stupidity

He couldn't find two St Bernards if they were in the same telephone kiosk as him.

And how many books have you heard in your entire life? The same number as Champion the Wonder Horse!
RED DWARF

He has an IQ of two, and it takes three to grunt.

He qualifies for the mental express line – five thoughts or less.

His brain is running on empty.

He's as smart as a politician is trustworthy.

He can talk to plants on their own level.

He's got a bungalow mind – nothing upstairs.

He's the world's only surviving brain transplant *donor*.

He fell out of the stupid tree and hit every branch on the way down.

When God was handing out brains, she must have been holding the door.

He couldn't pour water out of a boot with instructions on the heel.

In a battle of wits, he's a pacifist out of necessity.

Random Insults

People around him are at risk from passive stupidity.

God might still use him for miracle practice.

He is proof of Einstein's theory that there is no limit to human stupidity.

He's as happy as if he had brains.

His brain is suing for neglect.

He's so dumb, blondes tell jokes about *him*.

He's so dumb, his dog teaches *him* tricks.

He's so dumb he thinks "aperitif" means dentures.

He's so dumb he thinks "Nessun Dorma" is a camper van.

He's so dumb he thinks the English Channel is a TV station.

He's so dumb he thinks Thailand is a men's clothing shop.

He's so dumb he thinks a polygon is a dead parrot.

He's so dumb he thinks Sherlock Holmes is a housing project.

He's so dumb he thinks Johnny Cash is a pay toilet.

He's so dumb he thinks $E = mc^2$ is a rap star.

Stupidity

He's so slow he was three before he got a birthmark.

When he went into a think-tank, he almost drowned.

He could qualify as a houseplant if he learned to photo-synthesise.

His ignorance is encyclopaedic.
ABBA EBAN

What he lacks in intelligence, he more than makes up for in stupidity.

He has an intellect rivalled only by that of a cabbage.

His brain would rattle around in a gnat's navel.

He's so stupid that when he missed the Number 30 bus, he took the Number 15 twice instead.

He's so stupid that when he went to a movie and it said, "Under 16 not admitted", he went home and phoned fifteen friends.

He's so stupid he once ordered sushi well done.

He's so stupid he bought a solar-powered torch.

He's so stupid that when he heard ninety per cent of all crimes occur around the home, he went out.

He's so stupid he once asked, "What's the number for 999?"

He has a mind as empty as the sleeping pill concession at a honeymoon hotel.

She never lets ideas interrupt the easy flow of her conversation.
JEAN WEBSTER

She's so dumb that when she went to hospital to give blood and was asked what type she was, she told them she was an outgoing cat-lover.

He has dozens of books in his library and has finished colouring most of them.

He's not a complete idiot – some parts are missing.

He's not as dumb as he looks, but then again, that would be impossible.

Next-day delivery in a nanosecond world.
VAN JACOBSON

If brains were taxed, he'd get a rebate.

Warning: objects in the mirror are dumber than they appear.

Appearance

I never forget a face, but in your case I'll make an exception.
GROUCHO MARX

I've hated your looks from the start they gave me.

He looks like a talent scout for a cemetery.

The last time I saw legs like that, one of them had a message tied to it.

He was a tubby little chap who looked as if he had been poured into his clothes and had forgotten to say "when".
P.G. WODEHOUSE

He's a parasite for sore eyes.
He's so ugly, when you walk by him, your pants start to wrinkle.
MICKEY RIVERS

When he walks into a room, the mice jump on chairs.

He's so ugly his mother fed him by catapult.

He's so ugly they printed his face on airline sick bags.

He's so ugly that when he looks in a mirror, his reflection throws up.

I've seen healthier-looking corpses.

He is so short that when it rains he is always the last one to know.

He has a face that would stop a sundial.

In his case, if love isn't blind, it is certainly in need of an eye test.

Don't point that beard at me – it might go off.
GROUCHO MARX

He's so fat, when he gets on the scale it says, "To be continued".

He's so fat he's got the only car in town with stretch marks.

He's so fat he can't even jump to a conclusion.

He's so fat I had to take a train and two buses just to get on his good side.

He's so fat he could sell shade.

Appearance

He's so fat you have to take three steps back just to see all of him.

He's so fat I ran around him twice and got lost.

He's so fat that when he steps on the scale, it says, "One at a time, please".

He's so fat that if he put another two pounds he could get group insurance.

He's so fat, the whole stadium can talk behind his back.

He's so fat that he's the same height lying down as standing up.

He's so fat he wakes up in sections.

He's so fat he's got smaller men orbiting around him.

He's so fat he's a DJ for an ice-cream van.

He's so fat that he went to a fancy dress party in a white sheet as Alaska.

He's so fat he was born with a silver shovel in his mouth.

He's so fat that when his pager goes off, people think he's backing up.

He's so fat he has his own postcode.

He's so fat that when he goes to the zoo, elephants throw *him* peanuts.

He's so fat he hasn't seen his feet for six years.

He's so fat that when he goes to the movies he sits next to everyone.

He's so fat that when he sunbathed on the beach, Greenpeace tried to push him back in the water.

He's so fat that when he goes to the beach he's the only one who gets a tan.

He's so fat that he needs a watch on both arms because he covers two time zones.

He's so fat he has to get out of the car to change gear.

He's so fat they had to grease a door frame and hold a doughnut on the other side to get him through.

He's so fat he has to put his belt on with a boomerang.

He's so fat he's on both sides of the family.

He's so fat that when he was diagnosed with a flesh-eating virus, doctors gave him thirty years to live.

He's so fat his belly button's got an echo.

He's so fat that when he gets in a lift, it *has* to go down.

Appearance

He's so fat, he can be his own running mate.
JOHNNY CARSON

His problem is that all those square meals have made him round.

Looking at him, I've seen better-dressed crabs.

He's so ugly that when he visited a haunted house, they offered him a job.

He's so ugly that kids trick or treat him over the phone.

His face was filled with broken commandments.
JOHN MASEFIELD

He was such an ugly baby that his incubator had tinted windows.

A blank helpless sort of face, rather like a rose before you drench it with DDT.
JOHN CAREY

She can't be that two-faced otherwise she wouldn't be wearing that one.

He's got a face like a slapped bottom.

Why do you sit there looking like an envelope without any address on it?
MARK TWAIN

Random Insults

Don't look now but something died on your head.

He's got that faraway look. The farther he gets, the better he looks.

You look at his face and think: was anybody else hurt in the accident?

I can see you now, bending over a hot stove. But I can't see the stove.
GROUCHO MARX

He used to be quite athletic – big chest, hard stomach. But that's all behind him now.

He's so short that if he pulled his socks up, he'd be blind-folded.

He's a little man, that's his trouble. Never trust a man with short legs – brains too near their bottoms.
NOËL COWARD

He's got a smile like a crocodile with wind.

The last time I saw legs like that, they were supporting a table on *Antiques Roadshow*.

He looks like an unmade bed.

The last time I saw anything resembling his face, it was being wiped.

He's so hairy you could knit him into a pair of gloves.

Appearance

He liked his first chin so much that he added two more.

He looks like King Edward – the potato, not the monarch.
IAN HISLOP

He's so ugly that if his face was his fortune, he'd get a tax rebate.

She was so hungry for publicity that she would attend the opening of an envelope.

He had the sort of face that makes you realise God does have a sense of humour.
BILL BRYSON

His teeth are like stars – they come out at night.

He's so ugly he could make an onion cry.

He's so ugly his wife takes him to work with her just so that she doesn't have to kiss him goodbye.

I've seen better teeth on a worn-out gearbox.

The last time I saw a mouth like that, it had a hook in it.

Some people's looks turn heads; his turn stomachs.

If he wants to see a horror show, he only has to look in the mirror.

Had double chins all the way down to his stomach.
MARK TWAIN

Why don't you get a haircut? You look like a chrysan-themum.

He has a good weapon against muggers – his face.

He's a trellis for varicose veins.
WILSON MIZNER

Most people need a licence to be that ugly.

They've got a picture of him at the hospital – it saves using the stomach pump.

His face is used to frighten people with hiccups.

There's enough wax in his ears to put a shine on a Cortina.

A four-hundred-dollar suit on him would look like socks on a rooster.
EARL LONG

He's so ugly that when he walks into a bank, they turn off the surveillance cameras.

He's so ugly that when he entered a gurning contest, they said, "Sorry, no professionals."

His voice is even louder than his tie.

He's got a face like a picture – it needs hanging.

Appearance

His teeth stick out so much it looks like his nose is playing the piano.

His face was filled with broken commandments.
JOHN MASEFIELD

He is dark and handsome. When it's dark, he's handsome.

He has a great face for radio.

He had a winning smile, but everything else was a loser.
GEORGE C. SCOTT

He's so small he poses for trophies.

I've seen more hair on a billiard ball.

I remember him when he only had one stomach.

He's so small he's a waste of skin.
FRED ALLEN

That's an interesting jacket. Does Worzel Gummidge want it back?

My wife asked what it would take to make her look good. I said, "About a mile".
HENNY YOUNGMAN

I've seen healthier-looking faces on a pirate flag.

Is that his nose or is he eating a banana?

221

I've seen wounds better dressed than him.

He could swat flies with those ears.

No, there's nothing wrong with that tie except that it's not tight enough around your neck. You can still breathe.

He's so ugly that when he stands on the beach, the tide won't come in.

He's so ugly that when he was born, the doctor turned him over and said, "Look, twins!"

They say that travel broadens one. You must have been around the world.

He makes a very handsome corpse and becomes his coffin prodigiously.
OLIVER GOLDSMITH

He used to be a model . . . for gargoyles.

His ears are so full of wax you could stick a wick in and light them.

He must have had a magnificent build before his stomach went in for a career of its own.
MARGARET HALSEY

He's got ears like a hatstand.

Appearance

She has so many chins that she uses a bookmark to find her mouth.

What a lovely hat! But I may make one teensy suggestion? If it blows off, don't chase it.
MISS PIGGY

She's had her face lifted so many times that whenever she raises her eyebrows she pulls up her stockings.

Her face is not likely to turn on many voters. Except perhaps those who are members of the British Horse Society.
JOHN JUNOR

She is so conceited that she has her dental X-rays retouched.

She was a large woman who seemed not so much dressed as upholstered.
J.M. BARRIE

She's like the Venus de Milo – very pretty but not all there.

She's got bobsled looks – going downhill fast.

She was a curious woman, whose dresses always looked as if they had been designed in a rage and put on in a tempest.
OSCAR WILDE

She measures 36–24–36 . . . but that's her forearm, neck, and thigh.

One more wrinkle and she'd pass for a prune.

I've seen better-looking bodies at a car breaker's yard.

Her acne was so bad, blind people tried to read her face.
JOAN RIVERS

She has all the grace and elegance of a beached whale.

Her face looked as if it had been made of sugar and someone had licked it.
GEORGE BERNARD SHAW

She's got a face like a busted sofa.

Whatever look she was aiming for, she missed.

She was so bow-legged she couldn't stop a pig in an alleyway.

She's as pretty as a picture . . . by Picasso.

She must have stretched her mouth so wide by putting her foot in it all the time.

Body off *Baywatch*, face off *Crimewatch*.

She dresses like she doesn't have any gay friends.

She had not only kept her lovely figure, she's added so much to it.
BOB FOSSE

Appearance

She has a face like a million dollars – green and wrinkled.

Her eyes are like pools – sunken and watery.

Beauty may only be skin deep, but she's rotten to the core.

That's a nice top. There must be a Cortina going around without seat covers.
JIM DAVIDSON

They say a pretty face is a passport. Well, hers expired years ago.

You couldn't tell if she was dressed for an opera or an operation.
IRVIN S. COBB

She's so hairy it looks like she's got a herd of yak in her armpits.

The reason she reached the top is because her clothes didn't.

Her clothes look good, considering the shape they're on.

A perfect saint amongst women, but so dreadfully dowdy that she reminded me of a badly bound hymn book.
OSCAR WILDE

At Christmas I would rather hang her and kiss the mistletoe.

Her only flair is in her nostrils.
PAULINE KAEL

They said that dress looked much better on. On what? On fire?

Her hat is a creation that will never go out of style. It will look ridiculous year after year.
FRED ALLEN

The only reason anyone would call her a pussycat is that she's dyed nine times.

Nature played a cruel trick on her by giving her a waxed moustache.
ALAN BENNETT

She has a face that would fade flowers.

It's like cuddling with a butterball turkey.
JEFF FOXWORTHY

The only justification for calling herself highbrow is that she's had her face lifted so many times.

Just because it's your size doesn't mean you have to wear it.

She wears her clothes as if they were thrown on with a pitchfork.
JONATHAN SWIFT

Appearance

Some women are blonde on their mother's side, some from their father's side; she is from peroxide.

She was what we used to call a suicide blonde – dyed by her own hand.
SAUL BELLOW

When they said she had a face like a saint, they could only have meant a St Bernard.

She was at the beauty parlour for five hours – and that was just for the estimate.

She got her good looks from her father. He's a plastic surgeon.
GROUCHO MARX

Her figure described a set of parabolas that could cause cardiac arrest in a yak.
WOODY ALLEN

She was so ugly she could make a mule back away from an oat bin.
WILL ROGERS

Every time I find a girl who can cook like my mother, she looks like my father.

She is a peacock in everything but beauty.
OSCAR WILDE

She's had her face lifted so many times there's nothing inside her shoes.

She spends her day powdering her face till she looks like a
bled pig.
MARGOT ASQUITH

My wife has lovely coloured eyes. I particularly like the
blue one.
BOB MONKHOUSE

Age

Pushing forty? She's clinging on for dear life.
IVY COMPTON-BURNETT

He's so old his blood type is discontinued.

He's so old his birth certificate is in Roman numerals.

He's so old he was a waiter at the Last Supper.

He's so old he drove a chariot to school.

He's so old that when he was a kid, rainbows were in black and white.

He's so old that when he was in school there was no history class.

He's so old he can remember when New York City was just fields.

He's so old he can remember when the Dead Sea was only sick.

229

He's so old he can remember when the Grand Canyon was just a ditch.

He's so old that his back goes out more than he does.

He's so old that when he went to blow out the candles on his birthday cake, he was beaten back by the flames.

He's so old he's got hieroglyphics on his driving licence.

He's so old he was DJ at the Boston Tea Party.

He's so old that when he walked into an antique shop, they kept him.

He's sold that *Jurassic Park* brought back memories.

He's so old his birth certificate has expired.

He's so old he can remember when *Madam Butterfly* was still a caterpillar.

He's so old the candles cost more than the cake.

He's so old that it takes him longer to rest these days than it does to get tired.

He was either a man of about a hundred and fifty who was rather young for his years, or a man of about a hundred and ten who had been aged by trouble.
P.G. WODEHOUSE

If things get better with age, he's approaching excellent.

Age

She could age herself by twenty years just by telling the truth.

She may well pass for forty-three – in the dusk, with a light behind her.
W.S. GILBERT

Forty has been a difficult age for her to get past. In fact it's taken seven years to the best of my knowledge.

A wife of forty should be like money. You should be able to change her for two of twenty.

Euphemisms

His elevator doesn't go all the way to the top floor.

The lights are on but nobody's at home.

The radio's playing but nobody's listening.

He's a few sandwiches short of a picnic.

He's a few trees short of an orchard.

He's a few clowns short of a circus.

He's a few peas short of a pod.

He's a few guppies short of an aquarium.

He's a few feathers short of a whole duck.

He's a few spokes short of a wheel.

He's several nuts short of a full pouch.

Euphemisms

He's a few chapters short of a novel.

He's a couplet short of a sonnet.

He's one song short of a musical.

He's one span short of a bridge.

He's one tree short of a hammock.

He's two socks short of a pair.

He's a few crayons short of a full box.

He's a few links short of a chain.

He's a couple of slates short of a full roof.

He's a few chocolate chips short of a cookie.

He's a few pickles short of a jar.

She's a few beads short of a rosary.

He's a lettuce leaf short of a salad.

He's a burger short of a Happy Meal.

He's a goose short of a gaggle.

He's one colour short of a rainbow.

He's a cup and saucer short of a place setting.

Random Insults

His truck's a little short of a full load.

His golf bag does not contain a full set of irons.

His manual drive is stuck in reverse.

He's a calendar with blank squares.

He's a BLT missing the bacon.

There's nothing between the stethoscopes.

He lost his boarding pass for a higher plane.

He's a square with only three sides.

He's a statue in a world of pigeons.

He's operating in stand-by mode.

She types 120 words per minute, but her keyboard isn't plugged in.

He's pedalling fast, but he's not getting anywhere.

He's got plenty of bricks but no cement.

There's no grain in his silo.

Not all his dogs are barking.

He's knitting with only one needle.

Euphemisms

He smells the coffee but can't find the pot.

His teapot's got a cracked lid.

There's plenty of salt in the shaker, but no holes in the lid.

Perfect chassis, bad driver.

He's permanently out to lunch.

He's playing baseball with a rubber bat.

Full throttle, dry tank.

His receiver is off the hook.

He's a titanic intellect in a world full of icebergs.

He's a violin minus a bow.

His gavel doesn't quite hit the bench.

He's goalkeeper for the darts team.

A photographic memory, but with the lens cover left on.

His puzzle is missing a few pieces.

He's a wind-up clock without a key.

He's not the sharpest knife in the drawer.

Random Insults

He's not the brightest porch light on the block.

He's not the shiniest penny in the jar.

He's not the smartest suit in the wardrobe.

He's not the coldest beer in the fridge.

He's a dim bulb in the marquee of life.

He's a couple of blocks behind the parade.

He's half a bubble off plumb.

His brain waves fall a little short of the beach.

Not all cylinders are firing.

His back burners are not fully operating.

He is bandwidth limited.

He's having a party in his head, but no one is dancing.

He has been short on oxygen one time too many.

The picture frame is empty.

He gives a lot of bull for somebody that hasn't got any cattle.

He has a one-way ticket on the Disoriented Express.

Euphemisms

He writes blank cheques on a closed account.

His ski lift doesn't go to the top of the hill.

There's a kangaroo loose in his top paddock.

He's a man on a mission, but he can't find his dossier.

His clock doesn't have all its numbers.

There are too many birds on his antenna.

There are too many jokers in his deck and not enough aces.

His truck can't haul a full load.

The cursor is flashing but there's no response.

The gates are down, the lights are flashing, but the train isn't coming.

The wheel is spinning, but the hamster is dead.

He couldn't hit sand if he fell off a camel.

In the pinball game of life, his flippers are a little further apart than most.

He gets his orders from another planet.

He doesn't have all the dots on his dice.

Random Insults

He's all crowns and no fillings.

He's all foam and no beer.

He's all belt and no trousers.

He's all cassette and no tape.

He's all hammer and no nail.

He's all foliage and no fruit.

He's all icing and no cake.

He's all missile and no warhead.

He's all wax and no wick.

He's swimming in the shallow end of the gene pool.

He's reading from a blank disk.

His suitcase doesn't have a handle.

There's too much yardage between the goal posts.

He's not playing with a full deck.

His driveway doesn't quite reach the garage.

He's diagonally parked in a parallel universe.

He couldn't hit water if he fell out of a boat.

He only has one oar in the water.

His belt doesn't go through all the loops.

His antenna doesn't pick up all the channels.

His modem lights are on but there's no carrier.

His chimney's clogged.

Room for rent, unfurnished.

The cheese slid off his cracker.

He doesn't have all his cornflakes in one box.

His gene pool could use a filter.

He's a barnacle on the ship of progress.

He's driving down the road of life with the handbrake on.

He's four bows short of a string quartet.

He's a butter knife in a steak world.

He's a black-and-white mind working on a colour-coded problem.

Clever Comebacks

I'm busy now. Can I ignore you some other time?

When your IQ reaches fifty, you should sell.

I'm trying to imagine you with a personality.

Do you want me to accept you as you are or do you want me to like you?

It's a case of mind over matter – I don't mind because you don't matter.

I've only got one nerve left – and you're getting on it.

Sorry, but you're obviously mistaking me for someone who gives a damn.

Of all the people I've met, you're certainly one of them.

A guy with your IQ should have a low voice too.

Clever Comebacks

Moonlight becomes you; total darkness even more.

I've seen people like you before, but I had to pay admission.

A half-wit gave you a piece of his mind, and you kept it.

Any friend of yours . . . is a friend of yours.

I feel so miserable without you, it's almost like having you here.
STEPHEN BISHOP

You should toss out more of your funny remarks – that's all they're good for.

People can't say that you have absolutely nothing. After all, you have inferiority!

There's a bus leaving in a few minutes. Please be under it!

For two cents, I'd give you a piece of my mind – and all of yours.

All that you are you owe to your parents. Why don't you send them a penny and square the account?

I'd explain it to you, but your brain would explode.

Next time I see you, remind me not to talk to you.
GROUCHO MARX

Why don't you go to the library and brush up on your ignorance?

A rejection letter from MENSA wouldn't be too much of a surprise for you, would it?

You're a habit I'd like to kick.

Are those your own feet or are you breaking them in for a clown?

If you had your life to live over again, do it overseas.
HENNY YOUNGMAN

Good news: you are no longer beneath my contempt.

At the beautician do you use the emergency entrance?

Who is using the family brain cell at the moment?

Now do you see what happens when cousins marry?

Your conversation is like the waves of the sea – it makes me sick.

Who am I calling "stupid"? I don't know. What's your name?

They say space is a dangerous place . . . especially if it's between your ears.

What do you use for contraception? Your personality?

Clever Comebacks

I can hardly contain my indifference.

Don't be ignorant all your life. Take a day off.

How many times do I have to flush you before you go away?

Would you like some cheese and crackers to go with that whine?

People clap when they see you – their hands over their eyes.

Have you been shopping lately? They're selling lives at the mall – you should get one.

I have a warm place for you – not in my heart, in my fireplace.
W.C. FIELDS

I would like the pleasure of your company, but it only gives me displeasure.

The last time I saw a face like yours, I threw it a fish.

Nice perfume, but must you marinate in it?

If I said anything to offend you, it was purely intentional.

Who did your hair? The council?

How can I keep a fool in suspense for twenty-four hours? I'll tell you tomorrow.

Random Insults

I'd like to leave you with one thought, but I'm not sure you have anywhere to put it.

I hope you stay single and make some poor girl happy.

When I want your opinion, I'll give it to you.

Nice dress. Are you hoping to slim into it?

I hate everybody and you're next.

You're a difficult person to dislike, but I'm managing it.

I don't want you to turn the other cheek – it's just as ugly.

Are you breaking those teeth in for Desert Orchid?

Looking through my diary, I do have a window for you – to jump out of.

I didn't recognise you for a minute. It was one of the happiest minutes I've ever spent.

Well, today was a waste of make-up, wasn't it?

I'll try being nicer if you'll try being smarter.

You are validating my inherent mistrust of strangers.

I would insult you, but you're not bright enough to notice.

That's a nice jacket you're wearing. I wonder if it will ever come back in style?

When you get to the men's room, you will see a sign that says "Gentlemen": pay no attention to it. Go right on in.

If you can't live without me, why aren't you dead yet?
CYNTHIA HEIMEL

I think you should live for the moment. But after that, I'm not so sure.

Shock me, say something intelligent.

I'm not your type – I have a pulse.

There was something about you that I liked, but you spent it.

They say no woman ever made a fool out of you. So who did?

If I promise to miss you, will you go away?

Don't leave yet. I want to forget you exactly the way you are.

Nice jeans. Do they come in your size?

Please keep talking – I need the sleep.

What did you say? I can't hear over the sound of your hair falling out.

Random Insults

I don't consider you a vulture – I consider you something a vulture would eat.

Isn't such a tiny mind lonely in such a big head?

Many thanks for your note. May I recommend a good taxidermist?

I'd like to reach your mind but I have no idea where it's currently located.

I like your approach. Now let's see your departure.

Tell me, what holds your ears apart?

See, you should never drink on an empty head.

Don't look out of the window. People will think it's Hallowe'en.

Is that a beard or are you eating a muskrat?

Talk is cheap, but so are you.

I hear you're a ladykiller – they take one look at you and die of fright.

You're nobody's fool, but perhaps someone will adopt you.

Nice to see you on your feet. Who sent the derrick?

I'd rather have root canal surgery without anaesthetic than go on a date with you.

Is that your face or are you trying it out for an ugly sister?

Thank you, we're all challenged by your unique point of view.

If what you don't know can't hurt you, you're practically invulnerable.

Sit down and give your mind a rest.

I just don't hate myself enough to go out with you.

I know you like me – I can see your tail wagging.

Is your name Dan Druff? Because you get into people's hair.

Sometimes I need what only you can provide: your absence.

There are several people in this world that I find obnoxious and you are all of them.

No, of course you haven't put on weight. By the way, where's your jockey?

I know you say you'd go to the end of the world for me, but would you stay there?

I've had a lot to drink – you're beginning to look human.

Random Insults

Your point has been received, understood and ignored.

What is this, a meeting of the ugly convention?

You have everything a man could wish for, madam, including a moustache and rippling biceps.

Some people have called you a wit – and they're half right.

After hearing you talk, I now know that the dead do contact us.

Careful now, don't let your brains go to your head.

I refuse to enter into a battle of wits with you – I will not fight with an unarmed person.

I hear you're very kind to animals, so please give that face back to the gorilla.

Whatever is eating you must be suffering horribly.

Keep talking. One day you'll say something intelligent.

I would say you were handsome but my guide dog might disagree.

If truth is stranger than fiction, you must be truth.

What's on your mind, if you'll forgive the overstatement?

What's a nice guy like you doing with a face like that?

Go on, tell them everything you know – it will only take a few seconds.

I don't think you're an idiot – but what's my opinion against thousands of others?

When you go to a mind reader, do you get half price?

You're not yourself today – I noticed the improvement straight away.

I'd rather go swimming with hungry piranha than have dinner with you.

The more I think of you, the less I think of you.

Don't feel bad. A lot of people have no talent.

I'd like to give you a going-away present but you have to do your part.

Don't you have a terribly empty feeling . . . in your head?

Keep talking. I always yawn when I'm interested.

Don't you just love nature, in spite of what it did to you?

It's hard to get the big picture when you have such a small screen.

You bring joy to others, when you leave the room.

Random Insults

Sure, cream rises to the top – but so does scum.

Don't go to a mind reader, go to a palmist – I know you've got a palm.

You say you fear success, but really you have nothing to worry about.

I'd rather stick pins in my eyes than go out with you.

If I could afford the wood, I'd have your mouth boarded up.

You make me believe in reincarnation because nobody can be as stupid as you in one lifetime.

I didn't understand why they called it the "rat race" until I met you.

What do you look like with your mouth shut?

You must have a low opinion of people if you think they're your equals.

You used to be arrogant and obnoxious but now you're the opposite – obnoxious and arrogant.

Did your sideshow leave town without you?

I wish you were all here. I don't like to think there is more.

I'd like to help you out. Which way did you come in?

Great body. Too bad its only purpose is to stop your head floating away.

Have you considered suing your brains for non-support?

I can't seem to remember your name – and please don't help me.

Let me guess . . . you're the kid who pulled a silly face and it stayed that way.

I can't talk to you right now. Tell me, where will you be in ten years?

They say opposites attract. I hope you meet someone who is good-looking, intelligent and refined.

Some day you will find yourself – and wish you hadn't.

Are your parents siblings?

Your red shirt goes so well with your eyes.

Were you born stupid or have you practised hard?

How did you get here? Did someone leave your cage open?

Make a mental note . . . oh, I see you're out of paper!

Make somebody happy. Mind your own business.

Instead of being born again, why don't you just grow up?

As an outsider, what do you think of the human race?

I'm not trying to make a monkey out of you – I can't take the credit.

There's one too many in this room – and I think it's you.

I'm not as dumb as you look.

So a thought crossed your mind? It must have been a long and lonely journey.

Are you the first in your family to be born without a tail?

When I look into your eyes, I see the back of your head.

Please breathe the other way – you're bleaching my hair.

If I ever needed a brain transplant, I'd chose yours because I'd want one that had hardly been used.

Sorry if I look interested. I'm not.

Are you always so stupid, or is today a special occasion?

What has a tiny brain, a big mouth, and an opinion nobody cares about? – You!

Guy: Isn't it amazing? Every time I breathe in and out, someone dies somewhere in this world.
Girl: Have you tried using a mouthwash?

Actress: What do you think is my best side?
ALFRED HITCHCOCK: My dear, you're sitting on it.

LADY ELIZABETH DRYDEN: How can you always be poring over those musty books? I wish I were a book and then I should have more of your company.
JOHN DRYDEN: Pray, my dear, if you do become a book let it be an almanack, for then I shall be able to change you every year.

KATHARINE HEPBURN: I think I am too tall for you.
SPENCER TRACY: Don't worry, Miss Hepburn, I'll soon cut you down to size.

JEAN HARLOW: Is the "t" in "Margot" pronounced?
MARGOT ASQUITH: No. The "t" is silent – as in "Harlow".

NANCY ASTOR: Winston, if you were my husband, I should flavour your coffee with poison.
WINSTON CHURCHILL: Madam, if I were your husband I should drink it.

LEWIS MORRIS (after not being appointed Poet Laureate): It is a conspiracy of silence against me – a conspiracy of silence. What should I do?
OSCAR WILDE: Join it.

CLARE BOOTHE LUCE (stepping aside in a doorway): Age before beauty.
DOROTHY PARKER (walking through): Pearls before swine.

SINGER: You know, my dear, I insured my voice for fifty thousand dollars.
MIRIAM HOPKINS: That's wonderful. And what did you do with the money?

MRS PATRICK CAMPBELL (to theatre producer Charles Froham): Always remember, Mr Froham, that I am an artist.
CHARLES FROHAM: Your secret is safe with me.

EDITH SUMMERSKILL: Mr Cooper, have you looked in the mirror lately and seen the state of your nose?
HENRY COOPER: Well, madam, have you looked in the mirror and seen the state of your nose? Boxing is my excuse. What's yours?

OSCAR WILDE: Do you mind if I smoke?
SARAH BERNHARDT: I don't care if you burn.

ANON: I passed by your house yesterday, Oscar.
OSCAR WILDE: Thank you very much.

GEORGE BERNARD SHAW (inviting Winston Churchill to the opening night of *Pygmalion*): Am reserving two tickets for you for my premiere. Come and bring a friend – if you have one.
CHURCHILL: Impossible to be present for the first performance. Will attend the second – if there is one.

SAM WOOD (directing the Marx Brothers' *A Day at the Races*): You can't make an actor out of clay.
GROUCHO MARX: Nor a director out of Wood!

DUSTIN FARNUM: I've never been better. In the last act yesterday, I had the audience glued to their seats.
OLIVER HERFORD: How clever of you to think of it.

LABOUR MP: Must you fall asleep while I'm speaking?
WINSTON CHURCHILL: No, it is purely voluntary.

ARTHUR SCHLESINGER JR: I liked your book, Liz. Who wrote it for you?
LIZ CARPENTER: I'm glad you like it, Arthur. Who read it to you?

LADY: There are two things I don't like about you, Mr Churchill – your politics and your moustache.
WINSTON CHURCHILL: My dear madam, pray do not disturb yourself. You are not likely to come into contact with either.

ANON: I really can't come to your party, Mrs Parker. I can't bear fools.
DOROTHY PARKER: That's strange; your mother could.

KATHARINE HEPBURN: Thank God I don't have to act with you any more.
JOHN BARRYMORE: I didn't realise you ever had, darling.

OSCAR WILDE: I wish I had said that.
JAMES MCNEILL WHISTLER: You will, Oscar, you will.

FREDERIC LEIGHTON: My dear Whistler, you leave your pictures in such a sketchy, unfinished state. Why don't you ever finish them?
JAMES MCNEILL WHISTLER: My dear Leighton, why do you ever begin yours?

JAMES MCNEILL WHISTLER: Don't touch that. Can't you see, it isn't dry yet?
MARK TWAIN: I don't mind. I have gloves on.

LORD NORTHCLIFFE: The trouble with you, Shaw, is that you look as if there were famine in the land.
GEORGE BERNARD SHAW: The trouble with you, Northcliffe, is that you look as if you were the cause of it.

BESSIE BRADDOCK: Winston, you're drunk.
WINSTON CHURCHILL: And madam, you're ugly. Tomorrow morning, however, I shall be sober.

Shakespearean Insults

He's a most notable coward, an infinite and endless liar, an hourly promise-breaker, the owner of no one good quality.
ALL'S WELL THAT ENDS WELL

His kisses are Judas's own children.
AS YOU LIKE IT

His brain is as dry as the remainder biscuit after a voyage.
AS YOU LIKE IT

Is his head worth a hat? Or his chin worth a beard?
AS YOU LIKE IT

As from a bear a man would run for life, so fly I from her that would be my wife.
THE COMEDY OF ERRORS

His celestial breath was sulphurous to smell.
CYMBELINE

There's no more valour in (him) than in a wild duck.
HENRY IV, PART I

There's no more faith in thee than in a stewed prune.
HENRY IV, PART I

You might have thrust him and all his apparel into an eel-skin.
HENRY IV, PART II

[Your] face is not worth sunburning.
HENRY V

[You are] the scarecrow that affrights our children so.
HENRY VI, PART I

Sell your face for five pence and 'tis dear.
KING JOHN

You are not worth the dust which the rude wind blows in your face.
KING LEAR

He draweth out the thread of his verbosity finer than the staple of his argument.
LOVE'S LABOUR'S LOST

They have been at a great feast of languages and stolen the scraps.
LOVE'S LABOUR'S LOST

I had rather be married to a death's-head with a bone in his mouth.
THE MERCHANT OF VENICE

If her breath were as terrible as her terminations, there were no living near her, she would infect to the North Star.
MUCH ADO ABOUT NOTHING

May his pernicious soul rot half a grain a day!
OTHELLO

Would thou wert clean enough to spit upon.
TIMON OF ATHENS

A fusty nut with no kernel.
TROILUS AND CRESSIDA

He has not so much brain as ear-wax.
TROILUS AND CRESSIDA

Observe him, for the love of mockery.
TWELFTH NIGHT

Battle of the Sexes

Give a woman an inch and she thinks she's a ruler.

Brigands demand your money or your life; women require both.
SAMUEL BUTLER

The only time a woman is interested in a man's company is when he owns it.

A woman will lie about anything, just to stay in practice.
RAYMOND CHANDLER

He's been trying to drown his troubles for years, but she's too good a swimmer.

Women are like elephants to me: nice to look at, but I wouldn't want to own one.
W.C. FIELDS

No two women are alike – in fact no one woman is alike.

Men wake up as good-looking as when they went to bed. Women somehow deteriorate during the night.

The difference between a battery and a woman is that a battery has a positive side.

My wife and I thought we were in love but it turned out to be benign.
WOODY ALLEN

He and his wife were inseparable. Sometimes it took four people to pull them apart.

Women give us solace, but if it were not for women we should never need solace.
DON HEROLD

If you don't think women are explosive, try dropping one.

Anyone who thinks that marriage is a fifty-fifty proposition doesn't understand women or fractions.
JACKIE MASON

Women should be obscene and not heard.
GROUCHO MARX

I like women with gaps in their teeth. They are so damnably useful when it comes to scraping carrots.
PETER TINNISWOOD

There are three types of women: the intelligent, the beautiful, and the majority.

I haven't spoken to my wife for eighteen months. I don't like to interrupt her.
HENNY YOUNGMAN

Women are like shoes. They can always be replaced.

I like a man that wears a wedding ring, because without it, they're like a shark without a fin. You pretty much gotta know they're out there.
BRETT BUTLER

Men aren't necessities, they're luxuries.
CHER

The only time a man thinks about a candlelit dinner is if there has been a power failure.

Men are like bank accounts – without a lot of money, they don't generate much interest.

Beware of men who cry. It's true that men who cry are sensitive to and in touch with their feelings, but the only feelings they tend to be sensitive to and in touch with are their own.
NORA EPHRON

Men are like high heels – they're easy to walk on once you get used to it.

Men only have two faults: everything they say and everything they do.

The difference between Government bonds and men is that bonds mature.

The fastest way to a man's heart is through his chest.
ROSEANNE BARR

It takes only four men to wallpaper a house, but you have to slice them thinly.

Men are like car alarms. They both make a lot of noise no one listens to.
DIANA JORDAN

A woman without a man is like a neck without a pain.

The one thing you can be sure of about a well-dressed man is that his wife picks his clothes.

Commitment is what every woman wants; men can't even spell it.

Women want mediocre men, and men are working hard to be as mediocre as possible.
MARGARET MEAD

There are only two kinds of men – the dead and the deadly.
HELEN ROWLAND

A woman without a man is like a fish without a bicycle.
GLORIA STEINEM

Men are like mascara – they run at the first sign of emotion.

When God created man she was only experimenting.

I've finally figured that being male is the same thing, more or less, as having a personality disorder.
CAROL SHIELDS

My sister gives me the creeps – all her old boyfriends.
TERRI KELLY

Men are simple things. They can survive a whole weekend with only three things: beer, boxer shorts and batteries for the remote control.
DIANA JORDAN

There is one thing you can give to a man who has everything – a woman to show him how it works.

I don't hate men. I think men are absolutely fantastic . . . as a concept.
JO BRAND

Men like smart women because opposites attract.

Man is the missing link between apes and human beings.
KONRAD LORENZ

Only a man would buy a $700 car and put a $5,000 stereo in it.

Man is the only animal that blushes. Or needs to.
MARK TWAIN

A man's idea of helping with the housework is lifting his legs so his wife can vacuum.

Men are like placemats – they show up only when there's food on the table.

Women speak because they wish to speak, whereas a man speaks only when driven to speech by something outside himself – like, for instance, he can't find any clean socks.
JEAN KERR

The first time you buy a house you think how pretty it is and sign the cheque. The second time you look to see if the basement has termites. It's the same with men.
LUPE VELEZ

The difference between a new husband and a new dog is that a dog is always happy to see you and only takes a month to train.

There is, of course, no reason for the existence of the male sex except that sometimes one needs help with moving the piano.
REBECCA WEST

Around the World

Albania

Albania is a fascinating country, but I wouldn't want to go for the *whole* weekend.
ANON

Australia

A Portaloo in the Pacific.
ANON

In America, only the successful writer is important, in France all writers are important, in England no writer is important, and in Australia you have to explain what a writer is.
GEOFFREY COTTRELL

Melbourne is the perfect place for a film about the end of the world.
AVA GARDNER

Australia may be the only country in the world in which the term "academic" is regularly used as a term of abuse.
LEONIE KRAMER

Melbourne is the kind of town that really makes you consider the question "Is there life before death?"
BETTE MIDLER

I came to believe that it is a crime to think in Australia.
BETTE MIDLER

Canada

A country so square that even the female impersonators are women.
RICHARD BRENNER

The beaver is a good national symbol for Canada. He's so busy chewing he can't see what's going on.
HOWARD CABLE

Toronto as a city carries out the idea of Canada as a country. It is a calculated crime both against the aspirations of the soul and the affection of the heart.
ALEISTER CROWLEY

So this is Winnipeg. I can tell it's not Paris.
BOB EDWARDS

Canada is the boring second fiddle in the American symphony.
ANDREI GROMYKO

Canada reminds me of vichyssoise – it's cold, half French and difficult to stir.
STUART KEATE

Quebec does not have opinions, only sentiments.
H.L. MENCKEN

The year is divided into one day and one night.
W.W. READE

Gentlemen, I give you Upper Canada, because I don't want it myself.
ARTEMUS WARD

England

After a fierce hurricane hit Birmingham, local officials estimate that the storm caused £800,000 worth of improvements.

It is now so dangerous in parts of London that even the muggers go around in pairs.

I went to Morecambe for the week, but it was closed.
COLIN CROMPTON

Welcome to Hastings – and you are welcome to it!

The only good thing about Luton is that, with a motorway, a railway and an airport, it's easy to get away from quickly.

Nobody but a monumental bore would have thought of having a honeymoon at Budleigh Salterton.
NOËL COWARD

The only bright lights in Grantham on a Saturday night are red, amber, and green.

The English think that incompetence is the same thing as sincerity.
QUENTIN CRISP

I'll only set foot in Bridlington when Hull freezes over.

All Englishmen talk as if they've got a bushel of plums stuck in their throats.
W.C. FIELDS

Silence can be defined as conversation with an Englishman.
HEINRICH HEINE

English women are elegant until they are ten years old.
NANCY MITFORD

If you live in Birmingham, then being awake is not necessarily a desirable state.
TONY WILSON

France

The first thing that strikes a visitor to Paris is a taxi.
FRED ALLEN

If I were God and I were trying to create a nation that would get up the nostrils of Englishmen, I would create the French.
JULIAN BARNES

I ran out of deodorant in Paris and had to go all the way to London to buy a new stick.
DAVE CHAPPELLE

The French remind me a little bit of an ageing actress of the 1940s who is still trying to dine out on her looks but doesn't have the face for it.
JOHN MCCAIN

To watch a Frenchman pay for something is to watch him die a slow death.
ROBERT MORLEY

We can stand here like the French, or we can do something about it.
MARGE SIMPSON

The French have got a reputation for bedroom habits little better than a mink's.
MAE WEST

Why do the French have the onion and the Arabs have the oil? Because the French had first pick.

Germany

It should have been written into the armistice treaty that the Germans would be required to lay down their accordions along with their arms.
BILL BRYSON

German is a language which was developed solely to afford the speaker the opportunity to spit at strangers under the guise of polite conversation.
NATIONAL LAMPOON

German is a most extravagantly ugly language. It sounds like someone using a sick bag on a 747.
WILLIE RUSHTON

Ireland

The Irish are a very popular race – with themselves.
BRENDAN BEHAN

The Irish are a fair people; they never speak well of one another.
SAMUEL JOHNSON

The problem with Ireland is that it's a country full of genius, but with absolutely no talent.
HUGH LEONARD

An Irish homosexual is one who prefers women to drink.
SEAN O'FAOLAIN

You know it is summer in Ireland when the rain gets warmer.
HAL ROACH

Italy

The Italians' technological contribution to mankind stopped with the pizza oven.
BILL BRYSON

Venice is excessively ugly in the rain – it looks like King's Cross.
JOHN GIELGUD

I would love to speak Italian but I can't, so I grew underarm hair instead.
SUE KOLINSKY

Luxembourg

On a clear day you can't see Luxembourg at all. This is because a tree is in the way.
ALAN COREN

New Zealand

A country of thirty thousand million sheep – three million of whom think they're human.
BARRY HUMPHRIES

Pakistan

Pakistan is the sort of place every man should send his mother-in-law to, for a month, all expenses paid.
IAN BOTHAM

Scotland

Any cat with four legs and a tail in Glasgow must be a visitor.

The great thing about Scotland now is that if there is a nuclear attack it'll look exactly the same afterwards.
BILLY CONNOLLY

The difference between a Scotsman and a canoe is that a canoe tips occasionally.

The difference between a Scotsman and a coconut is that you can get a drink out of a coconut.

I have been trying all my life to like Scotchmen, and am obliged to desist from the experiment in despair.
CHARLES LAMB

It requires a surgical operation to get a joke well into a Scotsman's understanding.
SYDNEY SMITH

Switzerland

A country to be in for two hours, to two and a half, if the weather is fine, and no more. Ennui comes in the third hour, and suicide attacks you before the night.
LORD BROUGHAM

Since its national products – snow and chocolate – both melt, the cuckoo clock was invented solely in order to give tourists something solid to remember it by.
ALAN COREN

A nation of money-grabbing clockmakers.
NICK LOWE

I look on Switzerland as an inferior sort of Scotland.
SYDNEY SMITH

It has produced nothing but theologians and waiters.
OSCAR WILDE

Turkey

If you can imagine a man having a vasectomy without anaesthetic to the sound of frantic sitar-playing, you will have some idea what popular Turkish music is like.
BILL BRYSON

United States of America

I've just returned from Boston. It's the only thing to do if you find yourself up there.
FRED ALLEN

First prize: a week in Detroit. Second prize: two weeks.

To an American the whole purpose of living, the one constant confirmation of continued existence, is to cram as much sensual pleasure as possible into one's mouth more or less continually. Gratification, instant and lavish, is a birthright.
BILL BRYSON

I come from Des Moines. Somebody had to.
BILL BRYSON

When you tell an Iowan a joke, you can see a kind of race going on between his brain and his expression.
BILL BRYSON

America is the best half-educated country in the world.
NICHOLAS BUTLER

It is a scientific fact that if you live in California you lose one point of your IQ every year.
TRUMAN CAPOTE

New York is an exciting town where something is happening all the time, most of it unsolved.
JOHNNY CARSON

Californians have this thing about open space. They have lots of it – mostly between their ears.
PETER COOK

I do not know the American gentleman. God forgive me for putting two such words together.
CHARLES DICKENS

In Los Angeles, by the time you're thirty-five, you're older than most of the buildings.
DELIA EPHRON

Americans have two brains, one in the usual place, and the other where the heart should be.
MARLENE DIETRICH

Philadelphia is the greatest cemetery in the world.
W.C. FIELDS

North Carolina is the place you fly over on the way to Florida.
JOHN FLEISCHMAN

Man: I'm self-centred and obsessed with my physical appearance.
Woman: Really? I'm from Los Angeles too.
RICHARD JENI

I am willing to love all mankind, except an American.
SAMUEL JOHNSON

Never criticise Americans. They have the best taste that money can buy.
MILES KINGTON

If you're going to America, bring your own food.
FRAN LEBOWITZ

There are two modes of transport in Los Angeles: car and ambulance. Visitors who wish to remain inconspicuous are advised to choose the latter.
FRAN LEBOWITZ

New York now leads the world's great cities in the number of people around whom you shouldn't make a sudden move.
DAVID LETTERMAN

New York . . . when civilisation falls apart, remember, we were way ahead of you.
DAVID LETTERMAN

There's nothing wrong with Southern California that a rise in the ocean level wouldn't cure.
ROSS MACDONALD

It is not necessary to have relatives in Kansas City to be unhappy.
GROUCHO MARX

If, in New York, you arrive late for an appointment, say, "I took a taxi".
ANDRÉ MAUROIS

Nobody ever went broke underestimating the taste of the American public.
H.L. MENCKEN

Pasadena: a cemetery with lights.

Washington, DC, is to lying what Wisconsin is to cheese.
DENNIS MILLER

Pittsburgh is Hell with the lid taken off.
JAMES PARTON

America is a country that doesn't know where it is going but is determined to set a speed record getting there.
LAURENCE J. PETER

The national dish of America is menus.
ROBERT ROBINSON

Frustrate a Frenchman, he will drink himself to death; an Irishman, he will die of angry hypertension; a Dane, he will shoot himself; an American, he will get drunk, shoot you, then establish a million-dollar aid programme for your relatives.
S.A. RUDIN

The American male does not mature until he has exhausted all other possibilities.
WILFRED SHEED

Anyone [like Ernest Hemingway] who marries three girls from St Louis hasn't learned much.
GERTRUDE STEIN

During the winter Seattle residents don't get frostbite: they grow mould.

In some Chicago neighbourhoods, looking for a parking space is not unlike panning for gold.
GARY WASHBURN

Of course America had often been discovered before Colombus, but it had always been hushed up.
OSCAR WILDE

Wales

The best thing to come out of Wales is the M4.

I spent two weeks in Wales one weekend.

Wales is the land of song, but no music.
DAVID WULSTAN